Modern MOONLIGHTING

How to Earn Thousands Extra Without Leaving Your Day Job

Roger Woodson

CONTEMPORARY BOOKS

Library of Congress Cataloging-in-Publication Data

Woodson, R. Dodge (Roger Dodge), 1955–
     Modern moonlighting : how to earn thousands extra without leaving your
day job / Roger Woodson.
          p.   cm.
     Includes index.
     ISBN 0-8092-3144-1
     1. Supplementary employment.   2. Home-based businesses.   3. Self-
employed.   I. Title.
HD5854.5.W66   1997
658'.041—dc21   97-10749
                                                                              CIP

This book is dedicated to Adam, Afton, and Kimberley, the people in my life who make it all worthwhile.

Front cover photographs: right, copyright © Chris Ferebee/Photonica;
left, copyright © Peter Poulides/Tony Stone Images.
Cover design by Kim Bartko
Interior design by Mary Lockwood

15   14   13   12   11   10   9   8   7   6   5   4   3   2   1

Contents

ACKNOWLEDGMENTS

I would like to thank Jake Elwell, my agent, for arranging the opportunity for me to write this book. In addition, my parents, Maralou and Woody, deserve credit for encouraging me to blaze my own trail in life.

INTRODUCTION

Are your fingers tingling? If they are, don't worry about it; you've just picked up the most powerful book available for increasing your income with safety and security. Taking a moment to open this book might well be the single most important step you've ever taken toward financial freedom. It's true, this book can be your ticket to bigger and better earnings and a finer lifestyle.

If you are curious about making more money, you owe it to yourself to explore the world of modern moonlighting. Working a side job is not what it used to be. In fact, you can start your own business on a part-time basis and grow into a new career or into a business of your own that will allow you more freedom than you've ever experienced at a typical job.

A lot of people are making thousands of dollars a year in their moonlighting ventures. You can become a part of this current trend and cash in on your skills. What types of hobbies do you enjoy? Did you know that many hobby activities can be converted into moneymaking businesses? They can, and I'll show you how to do it. The income potential for you as a moonlighter is unlimited.

If you are wondering what you can do to offset the rising cost of living, you're holding the answer in your hands. It doesn't matter if you are a plumber or an artist, you can make plenty of spending money in your spare time. The work you do can be fun. Don't think that you are going to have to perform some menial task at minimum wage in an after-hours job. You could take this route, but there's no reason to when you have the power of *Modern Moonlighting*.

Moonlighting has changed. There was a time when working a second job made a person look or feel inadequate as a provider. This is no longer the case. Today's modern moonlighters are turning their time off into hefty bank accounts, new careers, and new businesses. There is no shame in working for yourself after the whistle blows on your day job.

Would you rather sit around the house watching television or make several thousand dollars a year in extra earnings? If you want to cash in on the time that you are presently wasting, this is your opportunity. With a little planning and determination, you can turn your life around and see rich rewards for your efforts. Maybe you will use the money to supplement your paycheck, or maybe you will find yourself the proud owner of a thriving new business. The power is yours, and this book is your guide down the path to prosperity.

As a business consultant, I've helped many people start and operate their businesses. My experience as a moonlighter has been diverse and successful. You can learn a lot from what you are about to read, and you might be amazed at how much money you can make doing what you enjoy. You really can have fun and make money at the same time. It's not difficult, and almost anyone can do it.

Take a few minutes to read over the table of contents. I'm sure that you will find topics of interest. Thumb through the chapters that follow to get a feel for the exciting opportunities awaiting you. It won't take long for you to realize that you are sitting on a mental gold mine. One of the first steps to financial freedom is a viable idea, and this book is loaded with tried-and-proven moneymaking ventures that can produce more income than you might believe possible. If the idea of making more money working a few hours a week as a moonlighter than you make at your regular job is appealing to you, read on.

ONE

ANYONE CAN DO IT

1

IS MOONLIGHTING RIGHT FOR YOU?

People have been moonlighting to make extra money for years. Times have changed. People still moonlight, but their options are much more varied and lucrative than they used to be. With the introduction of computers and virtual offices, it's possible to run a big-league business from your basement. You don't have to be in a high-rent district to attract generous clients. While technology has changed the way many people work, most of the old-fashioned ways of making money still are viable. When it comes down to it, there are so many ways to make extra money that it can boggle your mind.

Is moonlighting something you should consider doing? It depends on your personality and your financial needs and desires. Everyone can find some good use for extra money. Turning your spare time into spare cash by doing something you enjoy can be like having a hobby that pays for itself. With the right selection for moonlighting, you can achieve more than just money. Self-esteem can grow out of owning your own business. Recognition for what you do is sometimes the greatest reward of all. Money is certainly a primary reason for moonlighting, but it is not the only one.

Modern moonlighting can be fun and profitable. You don't have to be ashamed of what you do after normal business hours. In fact, you can be darned proud of your entrepreneurial enterprise. It was not long ago when people who held down two jobs were looked on with a different view. They often were considered something less than successful in their careers. Not so today. Starting your own business on your own time not only makes sense, it can also make a lot of money. And few people will have anything bad to say about you when you are the owner of a growing business.

In past years, a bank executive who needed extra money could hardly risk pumping gas or waiting tables at night. A banker's reputation could be tarnished by such work. So, what was a white-collar worker to do for evening income? Many possibilities existed, but nothing to match the endless opportunities afforded by modern moonlighting. Today, a banker could log onto the Internet and provide financial guidance for a fee. This would not have been possible just a few years ago.

So much has changed in our society that moonlighting is nothing like it once was. The concept is the same, and some of the old standby jobs still exist, but you are on the threshold of a new frontier. Don't think that you have to be computer savvy to take advantage of this New Age moonlighting. Computers can play a large role in your work, but they don't have to. Plenty of profitable ventures are just waiting for you to tap into them.

Is moonlighting right for you? Are you a candidate for moonlighting? Ask yourself these questions:

- Are you satisfied with your present financial status?
- Would your life be better if you had more money?
- Do you enjoy special treats?
- Have you ever dreamed of owning your own business?
- Are you willing to change your life for the better?
- Could you use an extra thousand dollars a month?
- Do you possess marketable skills?

- Does a life without financial limits excite you?
- Are you a creative thinker?
- Would you like to work from home with flexible hours?

Not everyone wants to work more than a regular eight-hour day. But if you are someone who wants more of the finer things in life, you may be a strong candidate for moonlighting. Whether you want to buy a boat or a mobile home, put your children through college, or live in a nicer home, modern moonlighting can be your vehicle to success.

Take a look at your present financial condition. Are you happy with it? Could it be better? Very few people are ever satisfied fully with their financial standing. Even if you make a good living at your regular job, you might enjoy picking up some extra money on the side to spoil yourself with. Buying a new camera or a new canoe could be reason enough to dabble in evening work. The amount of money that can be made from a part-time business may stagger you. Some people, and I've been one of them, make more money in a few hours of evening work than they make at their day jobs. This fact may surprise you, but it's true. Let me give you a few examples from my past to show you the type of earning power you may have in your after-hours work.

When I was much younger, I worked as a plumber by day. My hours were from 7:30 A.M. to 4:30 P.M. My weekly paycheck was pretty good, but I wanted to own my own business. This led me to my first serious moonlighting operation. After working a full day for my employer, I would go out and work nights and weekends for myself. My income on the side jobs was three times what my plumbing wages were. Certain expenses had to be accounted for, but I still made a lot more money. In less than six months, I had established my own plumbing business, and I've been self-employed from that day on. It was possible for me to make more money, on the side, by working a full day on Saturday than I made for a full 40-hour week with a plumbing company.

Once I established my plumbing business, I needed something else to do with my spare time. Photography was my favorite hobby, and I loved to buy all the best equipment. But, professional photo equipment is pricey. To justify my purchases, I decided to do some moonlighting with the gear. Way back in the 1970s, I could make $500 a day shooting a wedding. A couple of weddings a month kept me in spare cash and plenty of camera equipment.

After moving to Maine, about 10 years ago, I decided to teach some adult education classes. I wanted the experience for giving seminars, and the money offered didn't hurt my feelings. By teaching vocational plumbing classes two nights a week, I made nearly enough money moonlighting to pay the rent on the house where I lived.

My next moonlighting venture was writing. I started off with magazine articles and grew into books. In just a few months, I was making more as a writer, at night and on weekends, than most full-time workers make at their day jobs. Because you are reading these words, you must know that I'm still writing and I am enjoying a good income from it.

After building a new house a few years ago, I wanted to justify the high mortgage payment. My house is in rural Maine, on 25 acres. After assessing the property, my wife and I decided to breed dogs as a moneymaking hobby. With just four dogs, we can offset the cost of owning a large home on a nice piece of riverfront land. Living where we do doesn't cost us any more than what we would pay for an apartment. This is all because of the extra money we earned from breeding the dogs.

In an effort to keep my examples brief, I've just hit the high spots in my moonlighting work. There have been many other fields of endeavor for me, such as business consulting, real estate, and similar situations. My point is this: moonlighting the right way can change your life for the better. So, is moonlighting something you should consider doing? It probably is.

How Much Money?

How much money can you make moonlighting? It depends on what you do and how much of it you do. Making $1,000 a month is a realistic goal for many people. Individuals with special skills and determination can make much more. The most that I can remember making in a single month from night work was $10,000. Unfortunately, I can't produce that kind of money at night on a regular basis. But I can earn between $4,000 and $6,000 a month if I put in enough evening and weekend hours. I would say an average monthly income for someone with special skills who is willing to work hard would be around $2,000.

What if you don't possess special skills and have no chance of making big bucks on your own time? Many people feel this way. It doesn't take a lot of specialized knowledge to breed dogs. You do have to learn about specific elements of the job, but you certainly don't need a college degree to do it. My daughter, who is eight years old, has a breed of dogs that she is working with for college money. Her puppies can be worth $1,200 apiece or more. If her dogs produce only six puppies a year, she makes a nice income. Granted, my wife and I help her, but almost anyone with an interest in animals can take on breeding responsibilities. Many other fields of work are available that you can turn to if you don't have technical or special skills.

Security

What is security? Is it a weekly paycheck? For many people it is. It takes a special type of person to quit a safe, secure job and open a new business. That is, of course, unless the new business is a moonlighting enterprise. Moonlighting allows you to maintain the safety net of your job while you establish your own business.

Whether you keep your night work as part-time income or turn it into your full-time job, you're usually money ahead.

Because I've been self-employed most of my adult life, I don't associate security with an employer and a weekly paycheck. I believe that I create my own security. I do this by being creative and determined. A boss can fire me on a whim. If I'm my own boss, my success or failure is up to me. No one else is to blame. In more than 17 years of self-employment, I haven't let myself down yet. I've experienced recessions, boom times, bad times, and typical times without falling. Yes, I've stumbled now and then, but I've never quit, and I've never lost. Your first step into moonlighting could be the biggest step of your life. It could change your future in ways that you may not be able to imagine.

No Limits

There are no limits to what you can accomplish as your own boss, even if you are a part-time moonlighter. Have you seen the commercial on television where the woman has sold 300,000 mops? I hate that commercial. It makes me so jealous that I could just spit! Think about it. Someone sits around and dreams up an idea for a mop. Yeah, a mop! All of a sudden, there are hundreds of thousands of sales, which must translate into hundreds of thousands of dollars. I'm sure a lot of work went into the marketing, manufacturing, distribution, and other business elements, but how can you accept the fact that someone probably will become a millionaire as the queen of mops? Well, the best you can do is acknowledge the fact that it could have been you. This type of opportunity does exist.

Mops are not the only place to get rich. Antiques bring big prices. I recently saw where a piece of paper, written on by George Washington, was found in an old book and sold for more than

$300,000. Can you imagine how you would feel if you had bought that book at a yard sale and then discovered the valuable contents? This is an extreme example, but many high-dollar values are waiting to be captured by people with an eye for antiques.

Arts and crafts are other moneymaking possibilities. If you stumble across the right item, you could be on your way to fame and fortune. There's a guy making little stuffed animals and selling them by the thousands for $5 apiece. Even if you don't tap into a gold mine, the average profits from quilts, paintings, and other works of hand can be lucrative.

Anyone Can Do It

The good thing about modern moonlighting is that anyone can do it. Education is always important in life, but as long as you are good at what you do, you don't have to be one of the greatest brains of our time to make good money moonlighting. Physical disabilities don't have to stop you from realizing your dream. The woman with the mop deal didn't have to make them herself. If you can think, you can grow rich from your part-time efforts. What you have to do is examine your interests and skills to see what you have to offer the paying public.

A person who hand stitches quilts can, under the right conditions, sell them for big money. If you like to tie fishing flies, you might come up with the next Royal Coachman or Gray Ghost. This type of design, with some good marketing, could pay you handsomely for years to come. Obvious choices for moonlighting are those that are equal or parallel to what you do in your normal workday. Burnout, however, can be a problem if you do the same thing over and over for too long at a time. It is generally best to seek a moonlighting opportunity that is not similar to what you do at your day job. Unless, of course, you want to get into a full-time business for yourself within your area of expertise, as I did with my plumbing business years ago.

TRADE AND CAREER OPTIONS

Let's talk about some examples of various trades and careers and how they may point you in the right direction with your personal moonlighting program. Assume, for the moment, that you are a paralegal. This is a job that is held in high regard by most people. What can a paralegal do for supplemental income? There are two ways to address this question. One is to pull from your skills within your professional field. Another is to find a moonlighting proposition that draws from your experience and background, without requiring you to use your everyday skills.

Most paralegals are good at paying attention to details. They usually can type quickly. This skill opens the door to working from home as a keyboard artist. In other words, you could write résumés for people, type a variety of documents, offer your services as a notary public, and so forth. However, coming home to perform work that is similar to what you do all day could be uncomfortable, both physically and mentally. Suppose you dug a little deeper into your strengths.

Let's say that you are a paralegal for an attorney who specializes in real estate law. This position might make you a prime candidate for becoming a real estate salesperson. Your background in real estate law would certainly add to your effectiveness in working with customers and clients. Many home buyers are available only after business hours to tour homes. This is an ideal situation for a moonlighter. The money that can be made in real estate sales can be surprising. Depending on the region in which you live, the brokerage firm that you work with, and what you sell, it's possible to sign up a deal in one night that will earn you thousands of dollars. If you get your own brokerage license, the rewards are even greater, because you don't have to share your commission with a brokerage owner.

Now, suppose you have children at home and don't feel good about working all day and all night. What can you do? Children can be a catalyst for ideas. Cashing in on the children's market is not a bad way to make it big in moonlighting. Maybe you and your children could make crafts together in the evening. This activity both gives you something to do together and creates a salable product.

In our second example, let's assume that you are a bookkeeper in your full-time job. You could help small business owners manage their books at night. There is a big demand for this type of work, and it's something that you can do from home. Many moonlighting jobs can be performed successfully without ever leaving the comforts of your house. You could extend your services to include payroll services, typing, and other business functions.

For another example, you are a carpenter who builds houses all day. When you get home, you relax by going into your basement and playing with your woodworking equipment. Carving decoys and making children's furniture are two aspects of woodworking that you like best. This is a natural. With a little mail-order savvy, you can sell your decoys all over the world. You can even sell them via the Internet. As for the children's furniture, you can make and sell it locally, put it on consignment in stores, and take special orders. There truly is no end to what you can do.

A TRUE STORY

What you are about to read is a true story of a man I know. Up until a few months ago, this man was a schoolteacher who worked after-hours in the winter plowing snow for customers. He likes to dabble in woodworking. For whatever reason, he started building picnic tables and benches in his barn. He set a few of the pieces out in front of his house, and they started selling. Before he knew it, he was swamped with orders. It's only been a few months since he started selling the wood items he enjoys making, but he is fast becoming one of the largest producers of outdoor wood furniture in his area.

When I spoke with the man recently, he said that he was making more money doing what he loved in his off-hours than he makes at both of his other moneymaking jobs. His children and wife, who is also a teacher, have joined forces with him to keep up with the demand for his work. I consulted with him, as a business consultant, on setting up a corporation and similar business steps. In the past few weeks, he has added more people to his operation and is cranking out quality wood products for affordable prices. His success is almost unbelievable. What started out as a weekend hobby has become a very strong income producer for him. You may find yourself in a similar situation by the time you finish reading this book.

THE SELF-ASSESSMENT

The self-assessment process of choosing the best moonlighting option is often the hardest step for people looking to make more money. Far too many people underrate their capabilities. When I was a full-time plumber, I thought of doing nothing but plumbing. This is typical. People associate what they do for a living with what they are able to do on a moonlighting basis. Sure, you can do whatever it is that you do at your day job, but you can probably do a lot more.

When you want to establish a list of objectives for your moonlighting possibilities, you should not be inhibited by what you feel your career is all about. Doctors can be photographers. Parents can produce children's toys. Accountants can carve decoys. Bus drivers can play in a band. You must look at all your skills and interests to get the most out of your moonlighting.

If you cut and deliver firewood for a living, you don't have to do the same work at night. Maybe you're a great stand-up comic and don't realize it. I know an oral surgeon who spends his spare time performing in magic shows at parties and special events. He does it mostly for fun, but he also makes money doing what he enjoys. If an oral surgeon can be a magician, what can you be?

Once you decide that you like the idea of making an extra thousand dollars, or more, a month, you have to get serious about what it is that you are going to do. Are you going to take classes to become a taxidermist or a gunsmith? Would you rather be an evening reporter for your local newspaper? Maybe you would like to polish and do detail work on cars in your home garage. All you have to do is think about what you enjoy and then set your sights on achieving your goal. The good thing about moonlighting is that you don't have to earn a full-time income at it. You can, but you don't have to.

All you need to pinpoint your strengths is a piece of paper and a writing instrument. Find a quiet place to sit down and think. Start writing down everything that you enjoy doing. If it's fishing, write it down. If making model airplanes is exciting to you, make a note of it. Almost anything has some value to it. It will be up to you, with my help, to decide what has the most value and appeal for your new business.

If you are intimidated about going into business for yourself, consider taking a part-time job. A friend of mine, who is fairly wealthy, works in the local library several hours a week. He doesn't do it for the money. The man enjoys books and reference materials. He also likes working with the computers in the library. By working part-time in this way, he receives fulfillment that he can't get anywhere else. If you only make $100 a week from moonlighting, you still are thousands of dollars better off at the end of the year. Part of your self-assessment will have to deal with money versus enjoyment. Now, let's investigate various methods for you to pick your path from.

QUESTIONS TO ASK YOURSELF

Before you choose a moonlighting vocation, you must ask yourself many questions. When you ask and answer these questions, you should do so in writing. Keeping notes of your thoughts will be helpful immediately and later on. You should start with several general questions and work your way into more specific ones. To get you started, let's run through some of the questions here.

Why Do I Want to Moonlight?

The first question that you might ask is why you are interested in moonlighting. Money is the reason for most people, but it is not the only reason. Maybe you want to hone a skill you already can perform. Perhaps your idea for moonlighting is the result of wanting something more rewarding than your day job, in terms of mental appreciation. Some people moonlight because they get bored when they are not working. It is not unusual to have more than one reason for going into a part-time job or business. If you have multiple reasons for your desire, write them all down. Then put them in priority. Let me give you a quick example from my past.

When I decided to work part-time as a professional stock photographer, I had many reasons for doing so. My main reason was to fulfill a goal with my camera. After taking thousands of pictures, I needed something to spark me into taking more. Gaining acceptance from a major photography agent gave me that push. The second reason for wanting to shoot stock was to see my slides on the covers of magazines. Least important in my decision was money. I had three reasons for wanting to moonlight as a stock photographer, and I put those reasons into perspective. Your assessment sheet should reveal similar information on your goals.

How Much Money?

How much money do you want to make? What amount of money are you willing to invest, or risk, to start your part-time business? Both of these questions are important. If you are unwilling to invest any of your own money, you probably will have to seek moonlighting work from an employer. When this is the case, you narrow your options considerably. Putting your own money on the line allows you to do just about anything you want. There is risk, but it doesn't have to be great. We'll talk more about risk reduction in later chapters.

Knowing how much extra money you want to make will help you choose a moonlighting path. For example, you aren't going to make $4,000 a month serving hamburgers at a fast-food chain. But you could do it selling real estate, writing books, or in other areas of interest. If your financial needs and desires are low, you have more options for work than you would if your needs are high. Define how much money is enough, and the answer will help guide you toward a proper path in moonlighting.

Do I Want to Work from Home?

Ask yourself if you want to work from home. Working from home places some limitations on your moonlighting options. It's difficult to make much of a living as a seminar provider if you are not willing to travel. Giving seminars is a viable way to make a lot of money, but travel goes hand in hand with the prosperity. Bookkeeping services, on the other hand, can be run from home very easily.

When you are deciding about a home-based business, you must determine what your definition of working from home is. Does it mean that your office is in your home, but that you travel to do your work, such as an electrician would? Or will all your work be confined within the walls of your home? There is a difference, and it's one that few people, even business consultants, think to define properly.

What Can I Do?

You are certain to consider what type of work you can do. Don't be modest in answering this question. Many people have tunnel vision when it comes to evaluating their income possibilities, especially those who have worked regular jobs for employers over a long period of time.

I consulted recently with a man who wanted to move from bigcity life to a country setting. He was depressed because he thought there was nothing he could do to make ends meet in a rural environment. After we talked, I changed his mood and his mind.

The man, who worked as a manager in a citylike development, was looking for similar types of employment. Because of the remote location he was interested in living in, there were no openings in his field. However, he was skilled in automotive work, small-engine repair, handyman service, woodworking, and other areas that did not pertain to his present employment. After a while, he and I were able to create a plan, and two backup plans, for him to make the transition he wanted.

Like the man in this example, you probably have many skills and talents that you don't give yourself credit for. Dig them out and place some value on them. If you enjoy working with computer graphics as a hobby, make a few telephone calls and see what graphic artists are charging for their services. Take some classes, if necessary, and hang out your shingle. If you like doing needlework, check around to see how much is being paid for the type of work you do. It probably will surprise you. Always remember this: anything you do has value.

When Will I Work?

Ask yourself when you will be available for your moonlighting efforts. If you need to be at home with children who require attention, you might not be able to get started until late in the evening. Working in your home can ease this burden. Are you going to work nights and weekends, or just one or the other? Get your mind straight on how much time you are going to put into your part-time moneymaking machine. The hours that you are available will have a bearing on what you choose to do.

Growth Potential

Do you want a moonlighting enterprise with growth potential? Is it your dream to build a big business that will support you in your retirement years? Not everyone wants this. Some people prefer to keep their business interests small and simple. Before you throw yourself into a commitment, you should know where you want to go with it. What do you want a year from now? How far do you want to go in the next five years? Assess this situation carefully, for it is a crucial consideration.

Part-Time Jobs

Part-time jobs offer people guaranteed income and no financial risk. This is perfect for some moonlighters. While I prefer to gamble on my own abilities and cash in on bigger earnings, many people are content to work their hours for a regular paycheck. Whether you start your own business or pick up a part-time job is your decision. I can't tell you what will be in your best interest. The best I can do is show you the pros and cons of both approaches and let you decide. However, don't overlook the advantages of being paid by the hour by an employer.

The questions that we have just examined represent the types of questions you should ask yourself. They are not conclusive. You will have, or should have, many more questions in your assessment. But at this point, you may not know enough about moonlighting to ask the right questions. That's OK. We're going to change that with every chapter you read.

GET READY

I want you to get ready to experience a major life change. No, you're not going to lose your hair or suddenly develop wrinkles from what we are about to do. But the chapters that follow this one are powerful and they can change your life for the better. To get the most out of them, you should have a notebook or tape recorder close at hand. At the very least, be ready to dog-ear some pages and highlight some passages. What you are about to read is your step-by-step guide to making money in your spare time, doing something that you already enjoy.

2

WHEN YOUR HOME BECOMES YOUR PROFIT CENTER

When your home becomes your profit center, life as you have known it will change. It's inevitable. This change doesn't have to be a bad experience, but it can be. Before you set up shop in your home, you should consider many factors. Being in business for yourself and working out of your home can be extremely pleasurable. Knowing how to set yourself up and balance your act is the key to success, and this is what you will learn in this chapter.

Working from home is a dream for a countless number of people. Is it all it's cracked up to be? Sometimes, but not always. There is a lot more to being in business for yourself, even on a part-time basis, than many people realize. And working in your home can be much more difficult than you might imagine.

Over the course of my self-employment I've worked from home and from commercial office space. By the end of this chapter, you will have plenty of information to help you decide where you should work from.

Many people think that being in business for themselves is the ultimate freedom. Running your own business, however, is frequently much more demanding than holding down a job. Not only do you have to do all the work you would do at a job, you have to manage the business. For some people, like myself, the extra weight is worth carrying. But this is not true for everyone. You may find that you would be happier working a second job for an employer than you would be opening your own business. You have both options.

Just as there are tainted views of self-employment, there are also confused visions of working from home. There are, to be sure, many advantages of working at home. But there are also disadvantages. You may not have the self-discipline to work at home. Juggling household duties, children, and work responsibilities may place too much stress on you when your office is in your house. On the other hand, being able to work all day in your slippers and comfortable clothes has its advantages. There is no clear-cut answer that applies to everyone when it comes to turning your house into a profit center. The decision is a personal one. Knowing this, let's get into some specifics.

WHY RENT AN OFFICE?

Why rent an office when you can use a spare room in your home as your office? Some types of businesses don't do well unless they offer storefront exposure. Fortunately, numerous businesses can do just fine in the confines of a home. What you decide to do with your moonlighting time will have bearing on whether you need a formal office out of your home. Most moonlighting ventures can do quite well without commercial space.

When you work from home, your overhead expenses are lower, which is always an advantage. Being at home gives you the edge of working whenever you can, without losing time traveling to and from a commercial office space. Time is money, so all the time you save is valuable in one way or another.

When you start a new business, the money needed for start-up capital can be reduced by working from home. Here is another benefit. But some people just can't get into the spirit of working when they are at home. It can be tempting to cut the grass or do a load of laundry instead of doing your moneymaking activities. Taking a coffee break in your kitchen can result in hours lost from work. When you have a boss and a time clock to deal with, a ten-minute break usually lasts ten minutes. This is not always the case when you are self-employed and work from home. Just answering your personal telephone can destroy your work schedule. All these problems can be overcome, but you have to acknowledge them before you can fix them.

Setting up a home office can be very productive. Large corporations are seeing benefits by allowing some of their employees to work from home. If you have the right personality and discipline, a home office can't be beaten. The question is, "Are you a person who can perform well while working from home?" Your personal traits and circumstances will affect your performance in a home office. Some other questions to ask yourself about your office include:

- Should I rent an office?
- Can I be productive working from home?
- Will a flexible work schedule suit my personality?
- Can I gain more family time?
- Am I self-disciplined enough to operate my own business?
- Will I become a workaholic?
- How much start-up money will I need?
- What will my operating costs be?
- Do I need reserve capital?
- Is moonlighting something I want to do?

The Benefits

The benefits of working from home are numerous. Working from home allows people more flexibility in their work schedules. It's easy to step into your upstairs office and work for 30 minutes. If you had to drive into town to get to your office, you might spend more time commuting than you would working.

Moonlighters who have young children benefit from working from home in many ways. I fall into this category. When I take a short break, I can walk downstairs and spend a few minutes with my children. If I worked in a downtown office, I wouldn't be afforded this luxury. When I work late at night, I'm able to hear my children if they wake up from a bad dream. I couldn't do this if I moonlighted from an in-town office. Because I'm at home, I don't have to pay a baby-sitter to watch the children sleep. All I have to do is take a monitor into my office and keep an ear open as I work.

People living together without children also gain personal benefits from working out of a home office. When it's time for a break, you can steal a few special moments with your significant other. In many cases, couples can work together in a moonlighting effort. Individuals who live alone maintain an advantage by enjoying all the comforts of home surrounding their offices. If they want a dog to curl up at their feet as they work, it's possible. Flexibility is the key ingredient in working from a home office.

Some other tips to consider when starting your moonlighting business are:

- Establish a private space to work in.
- Define a work schedule and follow it.
- Confine yourself to minimum needs in the beginning.
- Don't spend your money on office gadgets.
- Consider leasing as an alternative to purchasing.

- Think about buying used office equipment.
- Cast a professional appearance at all times.
- Set up a working budget.
- Build a business plan.

THE DOWNSIDE

The downside of a home office can take many forms. Temptations to do things around the house, when you should be working, is one of the most disastrous for home-based entrepreneurs. This applies to full-time and part-time workers. The need to keep up with chores around the house can be a major distraction when you walk past them every time you come and go from your office.

In certain cases, working from home can present a poor professional image, although this is not as big a factor today as it once was. At one time people who worked from home were considered unsuccessful or just starting out. Today, you know you've made it when you reach the point where you can work from within your living quarters. Of course, image is a factor in some types of businesses, so your home must meet certain criteria if customers come to you.

You may find yourself becoming a workaholic if you choose to conduct business from your dining-room table. While there is an advantage to being able to slip work in during small windows of opportunity, you can become consumed by working all the time.

When you work from home, you may feel as if you have no private life. Your telephone may ring at all hours of the day and night with customers calling you. If this is the case, invest in a separate telephone line and install an answering machine on it to take your calls when the "office" is closed. A word of advice, turn off the ringer on the telephone and turn down the volume on the answering machine all the way. Otherwise, you may be tempted to listen in and pick up business calls when you are supposed to be relaxing.

I could go on and on with disadvantages of working from home. There are many situations that you must assess and resolve. But just as there are a number of disadvantages, there are also a host of advantages. Once you get started, you will get a feel for how it goes with your business. Then you can make adjustments to refine your system.

Working Around Your Children

If you have young children, working your schedule around them can be a challenge. It's hard to resist a child's urging to watch a movie or go outside and play when you know that you should be working. The ages of your children will have a lot to do with how you handle this potential problem. There are, however, many proven ways to keep peace in the family while getting your moonlighting done.

Try to find some part of your home, even if it is your garage, where you can go and sequester yourself to work. Having a closed door between you and your family is a step in the right direction. Impress on your family members that the door is not to be disturbed except for emergencies. Let your family know that this is where you work and that you need quiet time when you are in your office. This approach works for many home-based workers.

Depending on your personal circumstances, you might be able to involve your children in what you are doing. Let's say, for example, that you make wreaths, dream catchers, and other types of country crafts. You probably can do this while spending time with your children, and they may even be willing to help. This is the best of both worlds. You are at home, with your family, and making money from moonlighting.

When there is a baby in your house, you pretty much have to align your work schedule with naptime and bedtime. Older children often are willing to occupy themselves if you explain to them the importance of what you are doing. It helps to plan activities for the children in advance, so that they are busy while you are.

My son wants attention from me every time he sees me. And I give it to him. But I have deadlines to meet and he is too young to understand what a work schedule is. Fortunately, I built my house with an upstairs that has two offices, a bathroom, and a conference room. The entire upstairs is business space, and it has its own private entrance. I can literally leave my house and go to work in my office, without ever leaving my home. Most people don't have such convenient work-at-home conditions.

I didn't always have children and I didn't always have such a well-laid-out home office. There was a time when I did all my writing in the laundry room. In another house, I closed in the screen porch and made it a makeshift office to write in. During these times, I maintained an in-town office for my other business interests and used the home office mostly for writing and occasional paperwork. You can use your bedroom, your dining room, your basement, or maybe even your attic to hide away from the family and work. But you must designate some specific place as your office. It's the only way that you will consistently get your work done.

If you involve your children in what you do, they will learn business principles that will help them throughout their lives. Afton, my daughter, has helped me stuff and stamp envelopes for years. It's a game to her, and she likes to help her dad. She frequently asks to help me write my books. Her understanding of writing and book publishing is deeper than that of most adults. She writes her own stories and binds them on a bookbinder that I have in the office.

As my daughter has grown older, she has taken on many business interests of her own. The dog-breeding business that she is currently running is making thousands of dollars a year and teaching her sound business principles. Afton loves animals and is showing all the signs of a successful businessperson. In fact, she is more advanced in certain business matters than some of my adult clients are. You don't want to force your children to work, but if they show interest, the right guidance can give them a fine view of business before they ever reach high school.

SETTING UP YOUR HOME OFFICE

Setting up your home office can be a lot of fun. It also can be frustrating and expensive. It's all a matter of how you go about it. You probably don't need a mahogany desk, a $600 chair, or a copier that will produce 20 copies a minute and collate them. Your exact needs will depend on what type of work you choose to do. It is important that you don't get too carried away with all the glitz and glamour of being a business owner and spend all your money on bells and whistles. Buy or lease what you need, and save the rest of your money for advertising or operating capital.

Finding a Place

The first step in setting up your office is to find a place to put your work area. If you will not be meeting with customers or clients in your office, it's easier to find a suitable location. Certain elements are helpful in an office. Good, natural lighting is beneficial, but not crucial. Ventilation of some type is important. Floor space is a consideration, and so are electrical outlets and lights. An office space should have a door for privacy. Beyond these items, the rest is up to you.

I've known many people who work from their dining-room table. Some of these people have used cardboard boxes as filing cabinets and managed to control all their business activity without a dedicated office space. If you have the room to set up a permanent, separate office space, I suggest that you do so. Working out of boxes and juggling meals with work can get tricky.

Finding space for an office can be difficult, especially if you live in a small apartment or house. Over the years, I've come up with many ways to establish a formal work space when it seemed as if no such space existed. Here are some of the ways and places that you may find useful in flagging off your office territory.

In a small apartment, all of the bedrooms are occupied, and there is no dining room. The kitchen and dining area is small. Your living room is large. Where can you set up your workstation? It may be possible to squeeze it into a corner of your bedroom. The dining area is a possibility, but not a very good one. What are you left with? The living room. But you can't use your entire living room as an office. Suppose you purchased some office dividers, the freestanding type that are used to create office cubicles, and used a portion of your large living room? This would work.

Now assume that you are living in a small house. What types of rooms or areas might be suitable for office space? If the house has a basement, you should be able to carve out some space down there. Extra bedrooms work when you have them. A dining room can work, and so can a portion of a large kitchen. If the house has an accessible attic, you could convert a section of it to an office, although remodeling can get complicated. Garages can provide needed office space. Enclosed porches and sunrooms also can be used. I've even seen walk-in closets converted to offices.

Envision living in a house where there is absolutely no place to put your office. The house sits on a nice parcel of land, but you can't afford to build a room addition. What can you do? There are two good, relatively inexpensive options in this case.

Consider buying a preconstructed storage shed. A good, handmade, wood building of this type can cost less than $1,000. Depending on where you live, you may need to insulate it, and you will want to install electrical outlets, but the overall cost is very low when compared to that of a room addition.

A better idea might be to buy a recreational vehicle (RV). You can park it in your driveway and plug it into an outside electrical outlet—and you have an instant office with lights, plumbing, cooking facilities, heat, and comfortable furnishings!

I have used travel trailers as offices on two occasions. At the moment, I have a motor home that I use as a "field" office. Even though I have an extensive office suite in the upstairs of my home, I like to retreat to the motor home whenever I can. It's great to work in an RV. You are out of your house, but not by much, and you can feel mentally good about leaving the office to go home. And you can enjoy your "office" in recreational ways when time allows. Most RVs and motor homes are tax-deductible as a second home, so you may even get some tax breaks.

There are so many ways and places to create your office that you shouldn't have much trouble once you give various locations some thought. After finding the right spot, you have to decide what you need in your place of business.

Everything Except the Kitchen Sink

Some offices seem to have everything, except the kitchen sink, in them. And some even have sinks. Specific furniture and equipment needs are determined by individual business owners. You may or may not need a fax machine. While having a copier is nice, it may not be worth the expense. Some essentials, however, apply to most businesses.

You need a work surface, usually a desk. Buying a new office desk can set you back several hundred dollars. Want a cheap solution? Buy two, two-drawer filing cabinets. They don't cost much at discount chain stores. Go to a salvage store or building-supply center and buy a hollow-core, slab door. Lay the door over the filing cabinets and you have an instant desk that includes four filing drawers.

If you want something a little more presentable than a door on filing cabinets, check the used-furniture market. Used office furniture is much less expensive than new furniture, and there is usually an abundance of it for sale. Make sure that the desk you buy fits your needs. You might want a small desk, so that it will not take up as much of your office space. On the other hand, you may require a massive desk to handle all your equipment and supplies.

After figuring out your work surface, you need a chair. Office chairs can cost less than $50 or more than $500. Get one that is comfortable and affordable. If you will be doing keyboard work, make sure that your keyboard is no more than two inches higher or lower than your hands when your elbows are bent at a 90°-angle to avoid tendinitis and carpal tunnel syndrome.

Once you have a desk and a chair, you may not need anything else, but a telephone is normally needed to conduct business. You might want an answering machine. An intercom that links your office to the rest of your living space can be helpful if you have a family. Fax machines are becoming more and more of a necessity for many business owners. So are computers.

Be selective when you are outfitting your new office. Separate your needs from your desires. Buy only the items that you really need. Don't invest in extra equipment until you are bringing in big bucks with your moonlighting work. A lot of people go crazy buying office equipment and supplies. Avoid this, or you may not have enough money left to grow your business.

Should I Lease It or Buy It?

Office equipment, like most other things, has become quite expensive. And technology is changing so rapidly that what is state of the art today is obsolete in six months. Leasing may solve these problems and provide a business owner with some tax savings. So how do you know whether to lease or buy?

If I were sitting in front of you now, as a small-business consultant, I would ask you to divide your major office needs into two categories: dependables and everchanging.

When I refer to dependables, I'm talking about items that don't drastically change in less than a year or two. Your desk and chair would fall into this category. Filing cabinets are another example. When you are dealing with dependables, I would recommend buying them. In the long run, you will come out ahead.

Everchanging items, such as computers, copiers, fax machines, and other electronic gear, may lend themselves well to being leased. Depending on the service agreements you get, you may not have to worry about what you will do when an expensive copier breaks down. One big advantage to leasing this type of equipment is that you can keep current with new technology. Lease a computer, use it for a year, and then trade up to the current model.

So many types of lease agreements are available that you have to evaluate each one on its own merit. Some are great, and some aren't. Read the fine print carefully. In fact, have your attorney look over the lease agreement and service contracts before you sign on the dotted line. Modern business owners might want to mix their purchases with leases to reach a balance point.

SOFT SUPPLIES

Soft supplies, such as envelopes and letterhead stationery, are normally a part of any office. How you treat this side of your business can affect your professional image. Customers may never come to your office, but you probably will correspond with them by mail. Your letterhead and stationery, envelopes, and business cards all play vital roles in establishing your business image.

When you set up your business, create a good name and logo for it. A descriptive name usually is best. In other words, your business name should tell customers about the services you offer. Use a name such as Ann's Custom Kitchen Designs instead of Annie Enterprises. Design a logo that is memorable. You want customers to recognize your company visually, and a logo helps you achieve this. In time, your logo should be synonymous with your company name.

After you have determined your business address, telephone number, name, and logo, have your soft supplies printed on high-quality materials. Business owners who use generic, fill-in-the-blank business forms are seen as amateurish. Spend a little more money to get good paper products that will leave lasting impressions on your customers.

A BUSINESS PLAN

You should draft a business plan before you begin moonlighting. The plan doesn't have to be formal or complicated. A simple outline of what you will do, how you will do it, when you will do it, and what you want from it is enough to get started. It may seem silly to create a business plan for a small, part-time business, but it isn't. You need to carve some things in stone and set a direction to go in. Here is an example of a simple business plan.

You are an artist. It is your dream to make money by painting and creating works of art. After browsing in many gift shops, you have a lot of ideas of what will sell. A big moneymaker is wildlife images painted on slate, and creating these images is how you plan to start your business. You will obtain pieces of slate and paint a variety of animals, starting with endangered species, on the stone. OK, now you know what you are going to do.

Where will your studio be located? Your work doesn't require a lot of space, so you will work out of your spare bedroom, which can function as both a studio and an office. Your slate will be stored in the closet, along with your art supplies. A folding table and a chair will be your primary work space. Your business plan is coming together.

Because you work full-time as an office manager, you will paint one hour each evening and three hours on Saturdays. The rest of your time will be spent marketing your products and creating new designs and ideas. Marketing your products is part of your business plan.

How are you going to sell your work? It is logical to place your products on consignment with retailers who sell similar items. You decide to put your work on consignment in as many shops as possible. Newspaper, television, and radio advertising seems too expensive and inappropriate for your needs, so you investigate mail-order advertising. If you place ads in specialty magazines and offer a catalog of all your art projects, you might generate enough demand to warrant the advertising cost. Initially, you will test market conditions with consignment shops. Once you know which pieces sell well, you will move up to mail-order sales.

In this example, we have already covered the general basics of a simple business plan. You can take the procedure much further, and ideally, you should. At a minimum, detail enough specifics so that you can get on track and stay there. Bouncing from idea to idea is a dangerous way to start a business. Go through all your ideas first and then make a commitment to what you will do and how you will do it.

YOUR BUDGET

Another major consideration when setting up your office and business is your budget. How much money can you afford to invest, and where should it be invested? Defining a budget is easy; staying with it is not always so simple. As a part-time business, you may not need a lot of financial resources to get going. Many types of businesses require very little start-up capital. If you work from home and don't advertise a lot, your operating cost should remain minimal. Even so, you need a budget.

Different types of money are needed when running a business. The first classification is start-up capital, that is, the money you will need to get your business set up and off the ground. Once you are up and running, you need operating capital. This money pays your routine bills for things such as telephone service. Advertising money is usually needed in a business. Reserve capital—money that tides you over during cash-flow slumps—is another category of needed money. You also may want a fund for growth capital that will help your business expand. Depending on how meticulous you are, you can create many additional categories. However, the ones we have discussed are enough to get started with.

When you lay out your budget, set up headings for each category. Plug in numbers as needed to represent your financial estimates. If you are going to spend $200 a month on advertising, put it in your budget. Because you will be maintaining your full-time job, you may not need reserve capital. Go through each category and plan carefully for your financial security.

Getting into business for yourself can change your future. It can change your life and your outlook on life. Once you start moonlighting, you probably will notice a number of changes. Most of them will be good, but some of them may be disappointing. In the next chapter we discuss how modern moonlighting can change your life.

3

CHANGE YOUR LIFE—THE BENEFITS OF MOONLIGHTING

Can modern moonlighting really change your life? Absolutely! Working in your spare time can generate enough cash and opportunities to change your life forever. You can begin to buy the luxury items you've always wanted. Moonlighting can put your children through college. It's even possible to move out of the city and into the country with the money and security you create in a moonlighting venture. To get the most out of moonlighting, you normally have to start your own business, but you can accomplish a lot working for a second employer. No question about it, moonlighting can definitely put you on a new path toward happiness.

LEAVE THE CITY

A big topic these days is how to move from the city to the country. Entire books are written on this subject. People make it sound harder than it is to escape city life. Don't get me wrong, it's not always a cakewalk, but it can be accomplished without a huge amount of stress and financial disaster.

My wife and I left the city, in Virginia, to move to Maine almost 10 years ago. Our home in Virginia was on five acres of land, about 15 minutes from the city. Even though we lived in the country, our work was in the city. We had to put up with traffic and attitudes that you would not normally find in a remote, rural location. Being a country boy, I wanted to bail out for the mountains. My wife wanted to wander the beaches. After extensive traveling and long-winded discussions, we decided on Maine. Financially, the decision looked to be a poor one. Maybe one of the worst ones we could make. But we made the move.

When we left the city, we lost a good income. We were building about 60 homes a year, running a real estate sales and property management business, and operating a plumbing business, all at the same time. Throwing caution to the wind, we made a commitment and went for it, with very little money saved. Fortunately, we landed on our feet and prospered. Many people don't under similar circumstances. If you want to get out of the city, there is a safer way to do it.

You can start your moonlighting business with a goal of leaving the city in some set period of time. You should allow at least one year for the transition, but you may not need that much time. If you choose a good moonlighting enterprise, one that can travel with you, it's possible to build up your business in the city, while you're making good money, and then take it with you to the country.

When you are seeking employment at high wages, a city is usually the best place to look. The fact that the cost of living in a city can be outrageous offsets the higher incomes, but there is little doubt that cities are where the most, and best-paying, jobs can be found. As a moonlighter, you don't have to lose out on urban incomes. A mail-order moonlighter can work from practically any location. Computer moonlighters also have the ability to work from remote locations and receive the fees they would command in an urban area.

If your goal is to get out of the concrete jungle, you must select your moonlighting opportunity accordingly. For example, you might be able to specialize in grooming poodles in the city, but this is not something that is likely to pay big dividends in the country. Conversely, dog grooming, in general, could be a viable moonlighting venture in either venue. Watering plants in corporate offices can be a profitable moonlighting job in cities and in smaller towns, but cities offer the most opportunity. Cleaning offices and buildings can work in any location. When you are evaluating your moonlighting options with an eye on rural America, make sure that the options you weigh will work in an area with a smaller population.

SEEING INTO THE FUTURE

What do you see when you predict your future? Is the picture pleasant or terrifying? Many people who work at regular jobs don't have a bright picture in their future. The cost of living increases faster than most wages. I remember, in 1974, I bought a Toyota Land-Cruiser for about $4,000. At the time, I was making about $8,000 a year. Today, a similar vehicle would cost upward of $25,000. To be on a level playing field, I would have to be making $50,000 a year. If I were still working in a job like the one I had in 1974, my income probably would be less than $28,000. This would mean that the cost of a vehicle had basically doubled in comparison with my wage increases. Most people struggle to keep up with inflation. This is why modern moonlighting is so popular and so necessary.

Think about the cost of gasoline. I remember when, not so long ago, the price was about 25 cents a gallon. Now it's gone up by more than a full dollar, to $1.25 or more. It costs five times what it used to. Do you make five times what you used to make? Homes have increased in price at about the same rate. My parents paid less for their first home than what a used pickup sells for today. I paid less for my first home than what many cars sell for now. The fact is that prices are going up faster than the incomes of many people.

Moonlighting gives you an opportunity to get more out of life. You have to work more to get more, but the rewards usually are worth the effort. Whether you want to build up a nest egg for retirement, buy a boat, send a child to college, or buy your first home, moonlighting can unlock the door of opportunity. What you start as a part-time moonlighting operation could turn into a major corporation that will provide for you in the years to come. Let's look now at how your choice in moonlighting can affect your life at various intervals.

Extra Pocket Change

If you are looking for a little extra pocket change, almost any type of moonlighting can meet your needs. Working extra hours at minimum wage will generate some cash. But small amounts of money aren't likely to make you feel a lot better about yourself. Neither will this money get you over the hump that keeps you from reaching a higher goal. It can mean the difference between eating day-old doughnuts and meat, but it's not a lot for most people to get excited about.

Money for Goodies

Working after-hours to make money for goodies can be fun. The whole time that you are working, you can be thinking of what your efforts will produce for you. We have to work to maintain the basics of life, and it's not always pleasurable. But when you are working for a toy, the reward seems much more appealing.

What type of personal perk would make you happy? A car or a boat might work. Buying an expensive item or taking a lavish vacation can make you feel good. Spending the money to do it may, however, make you feel guilty. You don't have to feel bad about treating yourself to something nice when the money was produced by moonlighting. Mentally, it's easier to spend moonlighting money on nonessential purchases than it is to dip into the funds earned by a regular job. This is one reason why moonlighting is so popular.

Let's say that you want to buy a new vehicle. The payments on it will run, including insurance, about $400 a month. This is a lot of money for many people. But you can earn all of it, and more, by moonlighting at something you enjoy. You could get a night job sweeping floors, bagging groceries, or taking food orders. Any of these jobs would produce enough income for you to pay for the car. But you'd have to work a lot of hours and be away from home. Other types of moonlighting could produce more money in less time, even right from your home. It's easy to make money for fun things when you moonlight.

Going from Employee to Business Owner

One of the biggest changes in your life as a moonlighter is the transition from employee to business owner. Not everyone wants to do this, and many people who do want the change experience difficulty with the transition. As a part-timer, you can change gradually. There is a big difference in starting a part-time business and starting a full-time business. Your regular job is your security and safety net. If your own business doesn't work well, you still have your regular job. There is very little to be afraid of as a modern moonlighter.

Starting and operating a business of your own can be frightening. You must know a lot to do it successfully. We are going to cover all the business basics in the next chapter. You don't have to be intimidated about going into business for yourself. It's much easier than you might think.

Once you begin your own business, your life will change. Some for the better and some for the worse. How it changes depends on many factors, such as your personality and the type of moonlighting that you do. Even if you are moonlighting for an employer, your life will change. The fact that you are working extra hours affects your normal life. How big will the changes be? It's difficult to say, but I can give you some idea of what to expect.

Addictive

Going into business for yourself can be addictive. You may find yourself married to your new love of making money as your own boss. Family time can be hard to come by if you let your business consume you, and this can lead to problems with spouses and children. Watch out for the warning signs. If you think about business at all hours of the day and night, you are a candidate for trouble. When you and the people close to you talk about business more than your personal lives, you definitely are showing signs of addiction. When you lose all sense of personal routine, such as eating and sleeping, to keep up with business matters, you may be over the edge.

I've been addicted to work from time to time. I shake it off for a while, and it creeps back up on me. There is a difference between working seven days a week, 12 hours a day to survive, and in being a workaholic. Workaholics do it because they want to. They eat, sleep, and breathe business. You want your life to change when you become a moonlighter, but not in this way.

Sense of Self-Worth

A good side effect of going into business for yourself is the sense of self-worth that can come from it. Striking out on your own and doing your work well is a feeling that is hard to beat. The lumps and bruises you get, both mentally and financially, become a distant memory once you make it to the top. And getting to the top of a moonlighting business is easier than you might think.

As a moonlighter, you are working with a limited risk. Your chances of succeeding are very good compared to those of a person who quits a job and goes into business on a full-time basis. Working into your new business slowly allows you to make adjustments for problems and mistakes. Because you're paying your basic bills with the money earned at your day job, a few losses in the moonlighting business shouldn't take you down. Growing slowly requires patience, but it is the safest way to reach lofty goals.

Buy More "Stuff"

As a successful moonlighter, you will be able to buy more "stuff." This is very important to some people. If you want a new wardrobe, you can make it your goal. When you wish for a new car, you can make the wish come true with moonlighting. Earning hundreds, or thousands, of extra dollars a month is within your reach. You will have to expend some energy to do it, but you can make it happen.

Retirement

Retirement is a time in life that can be very frightening. Most people never are really prepared to retire. They reach a certain age and realize that they don't have enough money to sit back and relax. If you want to set a goal to retire at a particular age, you can use your moonlighting work to achieve your goal.

Money devalues quickly as time passes. Having $50,000 in the bank today may not help you much 20 years from now. The cost of living goes up, and interest rates are not always strong. Unless you make high-risk investments, you can't receive high returns on your money. Conservative saving for retirement is good, but it takes a lot of money, at today's rates, to provide a comfortable life for yourself in later years. Moonlighting can be the answer.

Many people are not able to save or invest much money at all in their retirement plans. It's hard enough just to pay the daily obligations of living. But suppose you could put away a thousand dollars a month for the next 20 years. How would that affect your retirement plans? With interest, your savings would be well over a quarter of a million dollars. Do it for 40 years, and you pass the half-million mark. Moonlighting has the power to give you a soft place to land when you no longer feel like working.

An Expensive Vacation

When was the last time that you took an expensive vacation? Have you ever been to Europe or Alaska? Would you like to soak up some sun in Hawaii? Most employees get one or two weeks of vacation each year. Even if they are being paid for their time off, they frequently can't afford to enjoy exotic places for their relaxation. You can change your life in this situation with just a little moonlighting. If you only make a hundred dollars a week from your part-time work, you can afford to take a cruise, fly to an exotic island, or explore the roads of America in a rented motor home. Your moonlighting profits can pay for some fabulous vacations.

Education

Education has become a very expensive necessity in modern life. Putting a child through college can cost close to $100,000 or more.

How can any average person hope to provide such an education for his or her child? Moonlighting is one way to hedge the odds. If you started making a thousand dollars a month as a moonlighter when your child was born, you would have in excess of $200,000, not counting interest or investment return, by the time your child enters college.

A New Career

You can create a new career with your moonlighting efforts. When you start a shoestring operation, it can grow into a major business. It's happened to other people; it could happen to you. There is no end to what your career possibilities may be. If you want to do something badly enough, you probably can do it by moonlighting.

Some businesses seem glamorous when you think of them. Others, such as cleaning services and pest control, don't seem quite so desirable. However, service businesses such as cleaning and pest control are moneymaking enterprises that could make you a millionaire, or at least provide you with a very comfortable lifestyle.

When you run down a list of potential moonlighting sources, you can get lost in the confusion. Opportunities exist for all types of people. Franchises can be bought with financing. You don't normally need a franchise to make good money, but it is one option. Most good franchises, however, are expensive and require purchasers to make substantial investments and still provide large sums of money for operating costs, so consider the huge investment if you think you want to own a franchise.

Look through the headings in the yellow pages of your local telephone book. See anything that strikes your fancy? What better place is there to search for income opportunities and new careers? Read *Entrepreneur* magazine. It offers advice on hundreds of income opportunities. You are not bound to whatever it is that you are presently doing in your job. With a little creativity, perhaps some training, and the aid of this book, you can be something altogether different in a very short period of time. Some benefits of moonlighting include the following:

- You can work from any location.
- You can build a hedge against inflation.
- You can get more out of life.
- You can be your own boss.
- You can indulge yourself in luxuries.
- You can change your life.
- You can retire earlier.
- You can build stronger self-esteem.
- You can afford a better education for your children.
- You can start a new career.

WORK HABITS

Your work habits generally will change once you go into business for yourself. People who work for employers sometimes develop routines, such as taking an hour for lunch every day. Do you require a full hour to eat a meal? Not likely. If you were working for yourself, you might just eat at your desk and keep punching out the profits. Getting a paid lunch hour is not going to happen when you are a business owner. You will get paid only for what you get accomplished, which is strong motivation to work harder.

Some people fall into the employee syndrome. They do what they have to do, but nothing else. This type of person may be capable of typing 75 words a minute, but he or she types only 50 words, because that is what the job requires. As an employee, it can be difficult to get rewarded for work that is above and beyond the requirements of a job. Many employers don't give bonuses for merit, so why work harder when others aren't? It's common to find employees working far below their abilities, because they will make the same money regardless of how much extra effort they put forth.

If you decide to go into business for yourself, you will receive no paycheck unless you produce. The more you produce, the more you make. Are you going to stare out of a window and daydream on your own time when you could be generating cash? If you are, you probably shouldn't consider operating your own business. Successful business owners stay busy. They don't sit around and wait for things to happen; they make them happen. There is only a thin line between some types of moonlighting and self-employment. Let me illustrate this with a short story from my past.

When I first moved to Maine, about 10 years ago, I set up a real estate brokerage firm. I hired a personal assistant and took on four other brokers to work with me. The assistant was the only person out of the bunch that accomplished much. Being new to Maine, I didn't know how things were done, but I found them to be very different from the way business was conducted in Virginia. The other brokers I hired refused to work nights and weekends, which is the time in Virginia when most agents and brokers showed property. People with jobs, the ones who can afford to buy property, often are available only after normal business hours. It seemed strange to me that local brokers thought a nine-to-five schedule was appropriate in the real estate business.

A sales professional has to make sales. It's unusual for sales to fall into one's lap. In fact, my motto is "Many real estate people show houses, I sell houses." A salesperson should not sit around waiting for a telephone to ring. Instead, the individual should be on a telephone drumming up business. Or better yet, be out pounding the pavement to find customers. After two years of operation, I was selling a higher volume of real estate alone than all my associates put together. I decided to downsize the company and work independently. The expense of paying for office space, utilities, and advertising for brokers who did not produce sales was too much for me to justify.

Some people simply don't have the drive to make things happen. They may be able to respond to work demands and meet required tasks, but they don't have what it takes to go the extra distance. When you go into business for yourself, you have to be willing to move out of your comfort zone. It is up to you to do it all. There is no longer a manager telling you what to do. You are your own boss. If you fail to assume the responsibility, your business will bust before it booms.

FALSE PERCEPTIONS

Many false perceptions pertain to self-employment. One of the largest is the idea that you, as a business owner, can do what you want when you want. There is some truth to this, but not so much as most employees believe. If your moonlighting is something other than a part-time job for an employer, you must think like a business owner. As a moonlighter, you might very well be a part-time entrepreneur. When you own your own business, you must dedicate everything you have to it. Taking off to go fishing or shopping in the middle of the day is a sure way to put yourself into a failing mode. It takes a lot of discipline to manage a business of your own.

Anyone who tells you that being in business for yourself is easy hasn't been in business very long. Owning your own business and calling your own shots is nice, but you have to pay a price for your freedom. The price comes in many forms. One thing that you are certain to run into is the need to work more hours than you would doing the same type of work for someone else.

As an employee, you are required to perform certain functions. Other people, such as managers and owners, take care of other business-related needs. To put this in perspective, let me relate to you what I went through when I opened my plumbing business.

Working as a plumber for an employer, I was instructed to do certain jobs at specific times. All my work was plumbing and remodeling. I didn't have to bid jobs, do job costing, plan advertising, run budget numbers, or manage the company finances. I was not responsible for collecting money owed to the company. I got paid even when the company didn't. As soon as I opened my own plumbing business, things changed. I had to do all the same types of work that I did as a plumber, plus, I had to run the business. The workload was heavy, and I had a lot to learn. Fortunately, I survived. Many new businesses fail within their first year.

Your advantage is that you are starting off as a part-time business. You can grow your work as you need to and as it is comfortable for you. When I started doing plumbing, I got into it as a moonlighter. This experience allowed me to work the bugs out of my business before I relied on it to pay all my bills. I suspect this is part of why I succeeded. It is important that you understand the new responsibilities you will take on as a business owner, but don't let them discourage you.

Another false perception about business owners is that they are all rich. Even though a full-time business owner may work 60 hours a week, there is no guarantee that wealth will be in the cards. Moonlighters often have certain advantages over full-time competitors. As a part-timer, your business will be smaller and more manageable than a full-time operation. Because you still have a job, you can afford to work for less than some of your full-time competitors. Many customers seek out moonlighters, knowing that their rates will be lower than those of established business owners.

Once you start talking to fellow employees about your plans for financial freedom, you are likely to receive tons of advice. Some of it may be valuable, and some of it probably will be worthless. You can count on hearing all kinds of stories. What you must do is take control of your life and make your own decisions. If you are influenced by others' talk, you might talk yourself out of going on your own. Or you may rush in with too much enthusiasm and not enough preparation. You are your own master when you become a moonlighter. What happens is, to some extent, within your control. Are you up for the adventure? The road can be rocky, but the rewards can be rich!

Beware of the Boo-Birds

Employees are accustomed to being told what to do, when to do it, and how to do it. Good employees follow instructions well. People who have worked for employers over many years often reach a point where they don't think a lot for themselves. They do what they are supposed to do and live quiet lives. If you start talking to coworkers about your plans to moonlight, you may get a variety of reactions and comments. Beware of the boo-birds.

As soon as you spread the word that you are going to open your own part-time business, some people will hit you with countless reasons why you will fail or why it is a stupid thing to do. Other people will try to convince you to do something that they have done or are doing. Watch out for people who try to enlist you in pyramid schemes or similar gimmick businesses. Believe me, you will hear a lot from friends, relatives, and coworkers when you announce your plans. Some of this information may be useful, but much of it may be destructive to your decision.

People who have not been in business understand very little about how a business owner really works. Many people have tried their hands at business ventures and have failed. Don't allow this to dismay you. The people who failed are not you. Succeeding in your own business will require hard work and dedication, but you can do it. Moonlighting is the perfect way to see exactly what you are getting into before you take the full plunge into self-employment on a large scale.

I've been self-employed for most of my life, but I've also done a lot of moonlighting. The fact that I own my own businesses doesn't prevent me from making money on the side. If my full-time occupation were building houses as an independent contractor, I could still take photographs in my off-hours, and I have. Some people are so attracted to the large amounts of extra cash generated from moonlighting that they find it difficult to give up, even when they are making more than enough money from their regular work. Modern moonlighting is one of the greatest opportunities available to you. To find out the business details of what's involved, all you have to do is turn to the next chapter.

Two

The Mechanics of Moonlighting

4
BUSINESS BASICS

We talked briefly in an earlier chapter about setting up your business. This chapter gives you a more comprehensive look at what is involved in starting and operating your own business. Many topics will be discussed. You will learn about making money with reduced risk. Using subcontractors will be discussed, as will administrative issues, marketing, advertising, and basic business structures. Consider this chapter your step-by-step tutorial to opening and operating a successful business.

There are many ways to run a business. Some are better than others. You may know people who break every business rule and succeed. But for every winner who breaks the rules, there are dozens of losers. Some aspects of business management are essential elements of success. People who open full-time businesses are more prone to spending the time, effort, and money to make matters right. Part-timers often cut corners or don't feel that they have to play by the rules, but you can get into just as much trouble as a part-timer as you can as a full-timer.

There are laws that pertain to business matters, and the penalties for ignoring these laws can be substantial. For example, if you hire an employee and don't observe the labor laws, you could wind up in trouble. Failing to pay your quarterly estimated taxes will result in financial penalties. Opening a real estate brokerage and mixing trust or escrow money with operating capital is against the law. There are a number of mistakes that can be extremely costly. The best way to avoid these problems is to be aware of your business responsibilities.

A BUSINESS STRUCTURE

One of your first responsibilities as a new business owner is to pick a business structure. You should ask yourself certain questions about your new business. These include:

- Should you incorporate your business?
- Is a partnership right for you?
- What's wrong with a sole partnership?
- Will a corporate structure protect you financially?
- Can customers sue a corporate stockholder personally?
- Is an S corporation the best type for your business?
- Do you need a lawyer?
- How much insurance do you need?
- Will you need to carry workers' compensation insurance?
- How will you insure yourself?
- Can you obtain business financing?
- Is it sensible to mortgage your home for your business?
- Can you obtain credit-card merchant status?
- Will you need employees?
- Should you hire an advertising agency to help you promote your business?
- What is a balanced advertising plan?

- Are radio advertisements cost-effective?
- How much risk must you assume?

Will you operate as a sole proprietorship, a partnership, or a corporation? If you choose to incorporate, what type of corporation will you set up? Most moonlighters set themselves up as sole proprietorships. This is a simple, inexpensive business structure that works well in many cases. You won't set up a partnership unless you have a partner. If you do need a partnership, the setup procedures are simple and inexpensive.

Corporations confuse a lot of people. There are misconceptions about what corporations can and cannot protect you from. I encounter questions about this frequently when I consult with people on business matters. So let's set the protection aspect of corporations to rest right now.

What is your understanding of corporate protection? Is it your opinion that by incorporating you can protect your personal assets, such as your money and your home? It's true that a corporation can shield your personal property from attack in some cases. However, there are a lot of situations in which being incorporated doesn't help you at all.

People frequently assume, incorrectly, that if they set up their business as a corporation, they cannot be held responsible personally in financial and legal matters affecting the corporation. In some instances this is true, but many times it is not. To illustrate the difference between the two types of situations, let's say that you are a licensed electrician. You have a day job and you want to do electrical work on your own in the evenings and on weekends. To start with, you will perform all the work by yourself. There will be no employees in your business. In this case, setting up as a corporation basically does you no good.

As an electrician who does all of the physical electrical work, your corporation can't protect you from liability. Insurance can, but your corporation can't. To set the stage for our example, assume that you went out the past weekend and upgraded an electrical service panel for a customer. Shortly after leaving the job, a fire started at the panel box. It was determined that the fire was caused by faulty wiring—the very same wiring that you had just installed.

Because you did the work yourself, the customer can sue you as an individual and the corporation as a business. The corporation was the contractor and you were the worker. In this situation, all of your personal possessions are at risk. However, if you had a licensed electrician on your payroll or working as an independent contractor, the scene would be different.

If you had sent out an employee or subcontractor to perform the physical work, your personal assets would not be under attack. The worker who did the work could be sued, and so could your corporation. But your home and personal finances would not be an issue in the suit. So if you are doing the work yourself, you can't hide behind the corporate veil. When you are using employees and independent contractors, a corporation can provide protection for you. Study what you've just read and commit it to memory. This situation is probably the question that comes up most often in my consultations during a business start-up or expansion.

Another aspect of corporations that affects many people is the tax consequence of incorporating. If you set up your business as a standard corporation, you will wind up paying what amounts to double taxation on your income. The corporation will have to pay income taxes on the money it makes. Then you will pay taxes on your personal income. This is not the case with a sole proprietorship, a partnership, or an S corporation. With a few exceptions, it is almost always best for a small business that is going to incorporate to do so as an S corporation.

When you are an S corporation, you file a tax return for it, but all taxes are paid on your personal return. You are only paying taxes once. There are a few limitations on who can set up as an S corporation. The types of things that prevent you from becoming an S corporation include the number of shareholders the corporation has and the percentage of money earned by the corporation that is passive income, such as rental income or book royalties. Check with a certified public accountant (CPA) to see what will be best for you in terms of taxes.

If you are going to be performing the work yourself, as most moonlighters do, a sole proprietorship probably will be your best bet. Setting up this type of business is very easy and inexpensive. Usually, all you have to do is go to your town hall and pay for a business license. If you are using a name other than your own, you normally will be required to file a doing-business-as (DBA) form. In a matter of minutes, you can be a legal business. Partnerships are not much more difficult to set up.

Corporations can be set up by individuals, but the procedure is more complex and time-consuming than it is for other types of business structures. I usually set up my own corporations, but my recommendation to you is to hire an attorney to do it for you. Attorneys will charge you several hundred dollars, but you will know that it is being handled correctly. If you set up your own corporation, you should be able to do it for less than $200, so you can save money by doing it yourself. It's not really difficult to do, but if you don't have experience in such matters, you could make a costly mistake.

You should consult with both a CPA and an attorney before you establish your business. These two professionals can help you enormously. Yes, they are expensive, but they usually earn their keep. You can get by without either of them, but you may be saving a few dollars now only to lose a lot of money later. Read books, such as this one, to develop informed questions, but then take those questions to local professionals who can guide and protect you. The business world can get messy, and it helps to have seasoned professionals pointing out the right steps to take.

INSURANCE

Even if you only work for yourself, you probably need some insurance. It just takes one mistake to ruin your life. Insurance can give you the peace of mind that you will not lose everything that you have worked for over some silly incident. Anyone can sue you for any reason. There's no guarantee the person will win, but there is always that chance. Protect yourself with adequate insurance. It can be expensive and you may hate paying the premiums, but it is a cost of doing business that you cannot afford to ignore.

What type of insurance do you need? This depends on what you do and how you do it. Liability insurance is almost always needed. You may need special insurance to cover your tools or equipment. Once you start using your personal belongings for professional purposes, typical homeowner's insurance doesn't cover much, if any, of it. Let me give you a couple of examples.

I use my camera equipment to illustrate books, to provide stock photography, and for occasional local assignments. It's not used professionally as much as it once was, but technically, it is still business equipment. If my cameras were not insured the way they are, my homeowner's insurance would cover $2,500 in losses from my home. Because I have well over $10,000 invested in the cameras and related equipment, $2,500 would not be much help in replacing them. And I need them to be insured when they are in my vehicles and on location. Therefore, I have an inland marine insurance policy that protects them at full replacement value, regardless of where they are when a loss is incurred. My computer equipment is also considered business property. It, too, is covered on my inland marine policy.

In my real estate business, I carry errors-and-omission insurance to protect me from liability. My plumbing business maintains a liability policy for any damage or injury caused on a job. A rider to that policy protects the plumbing tools. Thus, you may need a variety of insurance to properly protect yourself and your assets. Consult with a reputable insurance agency for advice. In fact, talk to several agencies before you make a commitment. I've obtained identical insurance from an agency for nearly one-third of the cost that another agency quoted me. Shop around, or you may pay much more than you have to for good coverage.

If you are going to hire employees, you probably will need workers' compensation insurance, which can be pretty expensive. If employees are closely related to you, such as your spouse or child, workers' compensation insurance shouldn't be required. Should you use the services of subcontractors, make sure that they carry their own insurance. Otherwise, you may be held liable for their insurance costs.

When people jump into business for themselves on a full-time basis, they give up the benefits provided for them by their past employers. This can mean not having health, life, and dental insurance. Because you are starting out as a moonlighter, you will be maintaining your present employment. Personal insurance may not be an issue for you. But if you decide to go full-time, be prepared to pick up the tab on all your insurance costs.

MONEY

We talked about setting up a budget in an earlier chapter, so we will just touch on the high spots here. As a moonlighter, your financial needs should be small. In any event, you need to establish a budget. Allow for start-up costs, operating capital, and reserve capital. Sit down and plan your finances. Some types of businesses require more start-up money than others do. For example, a dog breeder will have to spend more to get started in business than a bookkeeper would.

Don't get all fired up about moonlighting in some particular area of interest if you don't have the funds to make a go of it. Carefully look over your financial needs. Count every expense you can think of and build in a slush fund for expenses that you are not yet aware of. If you don't do this, your business may fail before it ever really gets going.

Business Financing

Obtaining business financing can be extremely difficult for any new business owner. It can be particularly hard to come by for a part-timer. If you want to borrow money, try to do it on a personal, rather than a business, basis. Once your business is established and profitable, you will enjoy much better luck in obtaining business loans.

Lenders who loan money to business owners want documentation and proof of profitability. With a new business, you won't have this. The best you can do is to prepare a drop-dead business plan that will impress your lender. Don't hold your breath while attempting this. It's been my experience that it is all but impossible to borrow money as a business until you can prove that you know what you are doing and that you are doing it profitably.

One way to start building business credit is to set up accounts with suppliers. If you are in a business where you need office supplies, ceramic materials, plumbing parts, or similar goods, try to open accounts for your business. Expect to sign for the accounts personally. Very few places will allow you to take corporate protection by signing as a corporate officer. Once your supplier accounts are established, used, and maintained for a while, commercial lenders will be more likely to approve your loans.

Taking out a second mortgage on your home is one way to obtain money to use in your business. Cash advances against credit cards is another way. Many businesses have been founded with money borrowed from friends and family. Private investors may fund you, but be careful when dealing with this type of lender. Have your attorney review and approve all agreements of this nature before you accept them. Chances are, you won't need a lot of start-up money, so this may not even be an issue for you.

OFFERING CREDIT-CARD PURCHASES

Offering credit-card purchases to your customers can give you a huge advantage over competitors, depending on the type of business you are operating. For example, a mail-order company that cannot take credit cards is at a distinct disadvantage. If you are making crafts and selling them at flea markets on the weekend, it is very helpful to be able to take credit cards, assuming that your goods are expensive enough to warrant financing.

There is a problem, however. It is more difficult than you might ever imagine to obtain credit-card status as a new, work-from-home business. Many providers will not allow merchants to accept credit cards until the merchant demonstrates a successful track record. It's kind of like getting a job right out of school. No one wants to hire you because you don't have experience. You can't gain experience until you have a job. It puts you in a no-win situation. Hang in there, though, it's not impossible.

When I lived in Virginia, I ran a major plumbing business out of my home. My annual gross was up in the hundreds of thousands of dollars. Yet no bank would issue me credit-card status. The reason was always the same. If I agreed to rent a commercial office space, I could take credit cards. As long as I worked from home, I could not. It's ridiculous. Why pay expensive office rent when you don't have to? Well, at that stage of my business development, I couldn't find a way around the problem, so I simply couldn't take credit cards.

Times have changed for me. I've grown older, wiser, and a bit bigger around the waistline. But I now can accept credit cards from two of my businesses, both of which I operate from home. The local banks gave me the same runaround I had received in Virginia. Maine bankers were no more sympathetic to my cause. I called mail-order people who offered credit card services for businesses. Guess what? The same story. No office, no credit cards.

After many frustrating attempts, I went to a savings and loan to seek credit-card status. And I got it! After getting it for one business, I went back in a few months and got it for another one. It was easy, and it didn't cost me much. The moral to this story is not to give up. Expect an uphill battle, but keep moving. With enough inquiries to enough places, you will find someone who wants your business.

How did I get credit-card status? Well, you might call it a form of blackmail. I offered to move all of my business accounts and personal funds to whichever lending institution would set me up with a merchant account for credit cards. This and my business plan and track record did the trick.

EMPLOYEES

As a new moonlighter, you probably will not be hiring employees right away. Think long and hard before you bring anyone in to work for you on an employee status. The minute you hire someone to work with you, many new considerations occur that may adversely affect your moonlighting. As an employer, you will be responsible for payroll, payroll taxes, workers' compensation insurance, and other duties and expenses related to employees. A business that can be very profitable for a single moonlighter might suffer financial losses when an employee is hired. It's true that employees should make money for their employer, but on many occasions employees may cost an employer money. Get your operation up and running in a financially healthy manner before you gamble on employees.

Many business owners don't feel successful until they have employees, but chances of success generally are much higher when you don't have employees. Use independent contractors instead or hourly employees whenever you can. This won't work in some job descriptions, but it does work in many. Subcontractors, independent contractors—whatever you want to call them—often are the most profitable way to expand your business.

Independent Contractors

Independent contractors are a business owner's option to employees. They usually are a great alternative. There are limitations to what you can use independent contractors for in a viable way, but they can be a much better investment than payroll employees. Let me explain what I mean.

If you hire an employee, you open yourself up to many things. There are labor laws to follow. You must maintain a quantity of employment records. As an employer, you have to contribute to the employee's earnings by matching payments for various payroll requirements. If you offer benefits, such as paid vacation, sick leave, health insurance, and similar goodies, you're paying for them. All of this adds up. Independent contractors normally, but not always, charge more per hour than a payroll employee, but the final accounting between the two types of help may not reveal much difference in cost. And independent contractors require much less administrative time than employees do. This is another time-saver and money-saver.

At the present time, I'm operating four successful businesses and I don't have a single employee. All my help is classified as subcontractors, because subcontractors offer business owners many advantages over employees.

The Advantages

Subcontractors are responsible for their own insurance. They don't ask for days off with pay, paid vacations, or other employer-funded nonproductive time. Independents are typically paid a flat rate for what they do. This means that you get what you pay for. Whether it takes two hours or ten hours for a subcontractor to complete a task, you are paying the same price.

You pay subcontractors only for what they do. You are not committed to paying an employee for 40 hours when there are only 30 hours of work to do. Because subcontractors are in business for themselves, the quality of their work may be better than that of an hourly employee. A business owner who works as a subcontractor can't afford to get a bad reputation.

Most subcontractors provide their own tools and transportation, an advantage that cuts down on acquisition costs and maintenance expenses for you. By paying what works out to be a higher hourly rate, you are subsidizing these advantages, but you know exactly what your contract obligations are. There should be no surprises. Subcontractors, because they are independent businesspeople, usually have more experience than many of the potential employees who are looking for jobs.

If you are looking for help in sales or manufacturing, you probably can take advantage of independent contractors, sometimes called pieceworkers. When you need someone for administrative work, you usually will have to go with a traditional employer-employee relationship. Look at what your needs are for help and weigh all the options carefully. If you can use independents, you may be better off. I've tried it both ways, and my profits are higher when I use subcontractors. This is not the case for all businesses. Don't rule out full-time employees. Look at all of your personal circumstances and then make your decision.

Administrative Issues

Administrative issues are the downfall of some business owners. Being organized is an important part of operating a business. If you are lax in your organizational skills and paperwork, there is a good chance that you never will be as successful as you could be.

Some people are better suited to administrative work than others are. I've known dozens of business owners who were excellent when doing what they did for a living. But these same people failed miserably when they had to take care of office matters. If your sideline is catering special events, such as weddings, you could be stunning in your ability to host a major bash and terrible at taking care of the paperwork. This is something that you have to watch out for.

Think of your business as working like your car. A car needs gasoline frequently to keep running. Oil is essential to the car's operation, but it is not added to the vehicle as often as gas is. Both gasoline and oil must be in a car for it to run properly. When it comes to your business, think of your work as gasoline and your administrative duties as oil. Your business won't run well without both elements.

If you don't have the inclination or ability to manage the administrative side of your business, hire a consultant, independent contractor, or an employee to manage the parts of the business that you are uncomfortable with. A number of moonlighters offer administrative services, so you shouldn't have any trouble finding someone to work with you.

Marketing and Advertising

Marketing and advertising usually make a business grow quickly. Word-of-mouth referrals are the best advertising you can get, but this type of exposure takes time to build. To get your business going quickly, you have to let a lot of people know what you have to offer.

Advertising is expensive. I have a saying about it though— "Good advertising isn't expensive at all, because it makes you money." It's the bad advertising that's expensive. What's the difference between the two types? One works and the other doesn't. The trick is figuring out how to come up with an advertising campaign that will work.

You can consult an advertising agency and have it design a campaign for you. Expect to spend a sizable sum of money if you choose this option. Some agencies are very good at putting together effective programs. Others are not so talented. If you are a do-it-yourselfer and don't want to spend money on an agency, you need to conduct some research.

Look at advertisements that are being placed by your competitors. Study what the ads say, how they say it, where they are placed, and so forth. Absorb everything you can about the advertising. What types of borders are used on the ads? How much white space is left in the ad? Are a lot of graphics being used? What are the strong selling points being pitched to consumers? Are television or radio advertisements being used? Continue this line of questioning until you have a good feel for what it is that your competitors are doing.

Once you get an overall understanding of competitive advertising, start to look at older ads. Go to your local library and search through old newspapers and magazines. Pay particular attention to ads that show up time and time again. Are they in the same media? Do the ads ever change? If you find an ad that has run regularly, unchanged in content, you can assume that the ad has worked.

Otherwise, the business owner would have changed it. An ad that has run repetitively in the same newspaper or magazine indicates that the media being used has been reaching the intended target audience of the ad. This type of research takes some time, but it pays off in avoiding wasted advertising expenses.

Flyers

Flyers are a fast and inexpensive way to get the word out on your new business. Going door-to-door with flyers is something that you can do after work, or you can arrange to have someone deliver them for you. Never place flyers in mailboxes; it is against the law. It usually is OK to put them in newspaper boxes.

I learned a tough lesson about flyers many years ago. Thinking I was brilliant, I went through a huge parking lot at a mall and stuck flyers under the windshield wipers of cars. Hundreds of flyers were distributed in this way. A couple of days after putting the flyers out, I received an official-looking envelope from the mall where I had blanketed the cars with colorful paper. The letter inside advised me to contact the mall office immediately to make arrangements for paying the cleanup costs associated with my flyers. Apparently, a lot of people threw the flyers into the parking lot. Thinking about it, I suppose the mall was reasonable in its demand. As it turned out, the mall waived the cleanup expense in turn for my agreement never to solicit there again.

Many people still put flyers on cars in parking lots. I've never done it again. Use your own discretion, but be warned, some property owners take soliciting very seriously.

Direct Mail

Direct mail can be an extremely effective tool. When you advertise by mail, you can pinpoint the recipients of your message. Renting a mailing list enables you to obtain a list compiled by demographics. If you want to reach only people who have new babies, you can do it. Income, age, education, hobby interests, and many other criteria can be used to develop an ideal mailing list.

Dozens of companies offer mailing lists. You can buy the names and addresses on peel-and-stick labels. Prices for these lists vary from company to company. Your selection criteria also affects the price. I normally plan on a cost of five cents per name when I'm working on a direct-mail program, but the names sometimes cost more.

Radio and Television

Radio and television can be effective in advertising your business. Rates for advertising on either radio or television are usually high. Most of this advertising doesn't result in immediate action. I consider radio and television advertising as a foundation for direct mail. Your company can build name recognition on the airwaves, and this is important in some types of businesses.

I've had success with television advertising on small, local cable channels. The work I've sought has been service-related, so a national campaign would not do me any good. Radio has never done much for my businesses, but it does work for some entrepreneurs. Don't expect television or radio to get the job done alone. Use them as a background for print ads and direct mail.

The Telephone Directory

Where do you look when you want to find a business that you need service or products from? The trusty telephone directory is probably the first place that you turn to. Keep this in mind with your business. People rely on ads in telephone books for quick reference. You should list your company in the telephone directory as soon as possible, because your listing may bring in new work and build credibility that your company is established.

You don't need to place a big ad in the telephone book. A simple line listing, given to you free when you obtain a business telephone line, often is enough. If you are going to work enough to make the cost worthwhile, however, a larger ad can produce more customers. You have to weigh the cost of the ad with the time that you have to spend on moonlighting. It is senseless to pay a high rate for a big ad and then have to turn away customers.

A Balanced Plan

A balanced plan is the most effective way to make things happen with advertising. You might use television, radio, print ads, direct mail, flyers, and billboards all as a team. Experts say, and my experience supports them, that a combination of various types of advertising works best. Let me give you an example of how I might put a balanced plan together.

Let's say that I want to start a home-building business as my moonlighting venture. A lot of money can be made here, and it is a job that I can do in my off-hours. To get customers, I'm going to advertise in many ways. First, I'm going to publish a press release in all the local newspapers that announces my new business. Most newspapers will print notices of new businesses without charging advertising rates.

My next step is asking radio stations to run ads for me during the morning and afternoon commuting time. Local cable television stations will run my commercials in the evenings. After a couple of weeks, I'm going to send direct-mail ads to people who live in apartments. They don't have a house to sell and they probably would like to own a new home, so they are good prospects, and my mailing list has been built around income requirements and rental status to ensure a good chance of success. I will place occasional ads in the local newspapers to round out my program. This is a good example of how several different types of advertising are used in conjunction with each other.

Reducing Your Risk

Reducing your risk is the best way to keep your business profitable. To do this, follow this business advice:

- Corporations don't offer full financial protection.
- S corporations are usually good for small businesses.
- A sole proprietorship can be very effective.
- Partnerships often lead to problems.
- You don't have to hire a lawyer to incorporate.
- Talk to CPAs and lawyers when setting up your business.
- Acquire adequate insurance coverage.
- Establish a business budget.
- Build business credit with suppliers.
- Become a credit-card merchant as soon as possible.
- Use independent contractors as alternatives to employees.
- Learn to run a solid administration in your business.
- Marketing and advertising are key elements to success.
- Good advertising is cost-effective.
- Direct mail can work wonders.
- A balanced plan is the most effective plan.
- Create a balanced business plan.

There is always some risk in what you do, but you can lower the odds of failure. The way to do this is with testing. If you think you have a good idea, test it. Many business owners have failed because they jumped in headfirst with ideas that they believed strongly in only to find that the public didn't share their feelings.

Testing is easy. Let's say that you carve duck decoys. Before you invest large sums of money creating a catalog and placing ads in national magazines, test your work on the local level. Carve a few decoys and see if shopkeepers in your area will buy them or take them on consignment. Find out which styles are popular. Once you know that your decoys sell well locally, you can branch out. Drive to a city in a different state and place your decoys with shopkeepers. After you receive a good cross section of response, you can formulate a national plan for sales.

Even when you first start and your business is tiny, keep risk reduction in mind. You will always be vulnerable to bad deals. Once your business grows financially, you can weather the storms better, but it is always best to avoid them. If you take the time to test your ideas before you launch major campaigns, you are much more likely to enjoy a healthy business.

Are you ready to start moonlighting yet? First, you need to decide what it is that you will do. The following chapters will provide you with plenty of ideas and details for choosing a good moonlighting career path. If you will turn to the next chapter now, we can start to unlock your creative genius.

THREE
FINDING YOUR NICHE

5
IN YOUR MIND'S EYE

Creative people don't always think that what they do has monetary value. But if you are a creative person, you probably can cash in on doing what you enjoy. Photographers, artists, and people who make crafts all have a chance to make money from their hobbies and interests. The amount of money to be made can be staggering. A competent photographer, for example, could make $1,000 in a single weekend by taking pictures at two weddings. Most of the moneymaking opportunities don't pay off in such large lump sums, but the revenue adds up over time.

Up to this point, we have been talking about moonlighting in general terms. We've covered the basics of setting up and running a part-time business. You have been prompted to think about what it is that you would like to do to make extra money. We are about to discover the specifics of probably hundreds of moneymaking opportunities, many of which have proved to be viable income producers. This chapter, the first on specifics, presents the creative outlets. Subsequent chapters will cover other types of moonlighting.

PHOTOGRAPHY

Photography, as mentioned previously, has held a special place in my heart since I was very young. My father wasn't too happy with my mother when she helped me buy my first 35 mm camera. He said that it was just a fad and that I would soon tire of it. It's been about 25 years or more since then, and I have not lost interest in photography. To this day, I still rib my dad about his comments on my "fad."

Lots of people enjoy taking pictures. Most of them have no idea that their work is salable or how much money they could be making while enjoying their hobby. Some ways to make money with your camera include the following:

- Studio photography
- In-home photography
- Wedding photography
- Pet photography
- Stock photography
- Real estate photography
- Commercial photography
- Insurance photography

Many photographers reach a point where they need some type of challenge. To satisfy mine, I started working on stock photography, weddings, and other moneymaking photo opportunities. The money was nice, but I did it for the fun and the recognition. Soon, I saw how much money could be made by moonlighting with my photo gear, and I became a part-time pro, complete with a major photo agent in New York. If you consider yourself a shutterbug, don't overlook your love of photography when contemplating a source of moonlighting money. In fact, let's break out some photo-related ways to make extra money.

A Studio

Many photographers feel that they need studio space to make money with their cameras. This is a misconception. Studio space in a commercial building is usually expensive. Getting enough work, on a part-time basis, to pay the rent and utilities can be hard. Established studio photographers and all the department-store types of portrait studios have changed the complexion of portrait work. Personally, I think you would be making a mistake by renting studio space. If you have a spare room in your home that is large enough to serve as a studio, then set it up. It's best if your house has high ceilings, but most homes don't. However, I think bigger money is waiting for photographers who leave the studio setting and go mobile.

In-Home Photography

I've done quite well over the years by offering my services as an in-home photographer. What does this mean? Simply that I take my equipment to the customer, rather than having the customer come to me, eliminating the need for a studio and raising the value of my services. Let me explain.

I'm sure you receive mail and see ads where you can go to a department store or chain studio to get dozens of pictures taken inexpensively. After more than two decades of photographic experience, I can see no way that these package deals are worthwhile to a pure studio photographer. The gimmick is to get people into the store and sell them enlargements and frames, not to mention any other purchases they may make while in the store. I don't think an independent photographer can compete in this arena. But you can provide certain options that the big guys won't. And this is where you win big.

As a traveling, in-home photographer, you bring the studio to your customers. Pack up your cameras, your lights, and your portable backdrops. Take them right to the doorsteps of your customers. How many photographers in your area are doing this? My guess is that it's not many. The advantages are easy to see. Children are more relaxed because they are in their own homes. Babies don't have to wait in long lines. People like to have items, such as pizza, delivered to them, so deliver your photographic skills and pull in bigger bucks.

As an in-home photographer, I've taken pictures of a variety of subjects. People, pets, insurance inventories, cars, antiques, and other items have all been on the list of my photo credits. This is a very low-cost way of doing business. If you already have your photo gear, the only new cost is film, transportation, and advertising. You can charge for your film and transportation, and the advertising expense is built into your fees.

I can't say that in-home photography is unique, but it is unusual. Not many photographers offer this service. If you do, the chances are good that you will receive plenty of work and a decent profit for your time. The fact that your service is convenient for customers makes it more valuable.

In-home photography is something that you can do in an urban or a rural setting. Your fees are determined by you, but the fact that you offer a door-to-door service adds to your value. The start-up cost is minimal, once you have your photo gear, and the profits can add up quickly. This may be one of the most dependable ways to make a good part-time living with your cameras.

Weddings

Weddings may well be one of the most profitable ways to make money with a camera in your area. Photographing portraits and portfolios can pay well, but I've never found a local source of income from photography that rivals weddings except commercial photography, and these jobs are hard to find. Weddings are easy to tap into.

Wedding photographers often use video cameras and still cameras. A medium-format camera is standard equipment, but I've shot a lot of weddings with 35 mm equipment. People who are shopping for a wedding photographer fall into many categories, and their budgets are as varied as their interests. You can fill some voids here, and fill your bank account at the same time.

As a wedding photographer, I've offered two types of service. In one case, I shoot the wedding for a flat fee and turn the negatives over to the customers. People like this a lot. It is not the traditional way of covering weddings, but it works and your deal is fast and easy. For example, you might charge $250 to shoot a set number of photos at a wedding and reception. The customer pays extra for all the film used. When the shoot is finished, your work is completed. The customers have the film printed and you are on to your next moonlighting job.

A more common way of handling weddings is to charge an hourly or flat-rate fee for your time on the job. Then you sell prints of your negatives (the negatives remain your property). In addition, you sell a complete line of photo albums, frames, and gadgets. A single wedding photographed this way can produce in excess of $500. You will have spent maybe half a day on the job and walked away with what is a week's salary for many people. Not a bad deal. And again, the start-up cost is minimal. People get married in all areas of the country, so it doesn't matter if you want to work in the country or in the city.

Pet Photos

Pet photos can become a specialty. Many photographers don't want to deal with animals. If you like animals, you can make good money taking their pictures. Pets are a constant source of revenue, but they are not the only animals that are profitable to photograph. Attend dog shows, cat shows, and horse shows. Even county fairs are a good place to drum up business. People will pay you handsomely for quality portraits of their animals. Buy a box of business cards, get a business license and some insurance, and you're all set to go with your existing camera gear.

Stock Photography

Stock photography is a numbers game. You can act as your own agent or acquire the services of an established agency. Stock agencies don't care about your education or your track record. They make their decisions whether to represent you based on your performance. If you can provide them with professional-quality images, you can be signed by an agent. Don't expect to get rich, though. You have to place thousands of pictures on file each year to make money with most stock agencies. There can be big money for years to come from stock photography, but it will not produce a regular stream of income like local service photography will. You can find stock agencies in a number of directories. Check with the reference section of your local library for listings. Be prepared to send several hundred photos for review before you contact an agency.

If you want to sell your own stock photography, solicit magazines, book publishers, trade publications, and even newspapers. This is a hard row to hoe, and it is not one that I would recommend when you are just getting started. Make your moonlighting money with service photography and keep stock work as a potential profit maker down the road.

Real Estate Photography

Real estate brokers need pictures of houses that they are trying to sell. Many brokers take their own pictures, but the quality is often poor. You can solicit real estate brokerages in your area as customers for custom photographs of professional quality. There's not big money in this, but it all adds up.

Commercial Photography

Commercial photography is hard to break into. It pays extremely well, so there is a lot of competition. The type of photography needed runs the gamut from advertising to recordation. You might be taking close-ups of a product in one session and press photos of executives in the next. Much of this work is shot in large studios and with expensive equipment. This is a good goal to work toward, but it probably is not an ideal place to launch your photo business.

A Photo Stand

You can take stock photos and sell the images over and over again at a photo stand. You can set up a stand at flea markets, fairs, special events, or anywhere where people congregate. At a rodeo I attended, a photographer set up a stand where he was selling bull-riding photos for $35 apiece. He sold pictures before the rodeo, at the intermission, and after the rodeo. During the bull riding, he was on the scene taking new pictures to sell.

You don't have to take pictures of bull riding to make money. Photograph gorgeous images of lighthouses, covered bridges, wildlife, flowers, or other desirable subjects. Take your show on the road. Set up in malls or wherever you can gain permission and show off your work. People will buy your pictures, and you can make hundreds of dollars a day doing this. It's simple, low-impact, and profitable, but you probably will have to travel on weekends to make the most of it. But what could be better than taking weekend trips and getting paid for it?

If you have camera equipment and the skills needed to produce quality pictures, you can sell your services and products easily.

Make calendars and sell them. Create posters—they're always popular. A cute, cuddly kitten in a poster is a sure sale. There is no limit to what you can do with your photographic interests when you turn them into moonlighting money.

WRITING AND PUBLISHING

Writing and publishing have been kind to me. My writing started out as a hobby and turned into a full-time career. I went from making a few hundred dollars a month with magazine articles to making in excess of $75,000 a year. Even as a part-timer, I was able to produce more than $20,000 a year while maintaining full-time work in another area of expertise. Some ways to make money writing include:

- Books
- Magazine articles
- Newspaper articles
- Résumés
- Work-for-hire assignments
- Business letters
- Advertising copy
- Annual reports
- Company policies
- Brochures

Not everyone has what it takes to be a moneymaking writer. I never thought I did. My work is all nonfiction, and it is based largely on do-it-yourself books that are written from my experiences. My background doesn't include fancy college degrees or even a strong knowledge of grammar. Publishers are willing to pay for firsthand experience that can be delivered in a reader-friendly way. The money can be quite good once you become established in the field.

My first book advance was $1,500. I was elated. In fact, I probably would have paid the publisher to put the book into print. Nowadays, I receive nearly 10 times what I used to in advances, and the semiannual royalty checks amount to what many people consider a full-time income. The written word is profitable.

You can start on your writing career quickly if you play your cards right. Don't look for big paydays right away. My first magazine article didn't pay anything, but it got me published. With each published piece, I gained confidence and credibility. Write for a local newsletter or newspaper. Send article ideas to smaller, less well-known trade journals and magazines. Write on subjects that you know and love. Your feelings will come through in your writing, and that is what sells.

Move up the publishing ladder to magazines, and then sell a nonfiction book on a subject that you know intimately. Let's assume that you are an avid gardener. This is a wonderful field to write about. There are many gardening magazines, and a lot of book publishers maintain long lists of gardening titles. When you write, don't try to reinvent the wheel. You don't have to have a brand-new idea, just a new spin on an old idea. Publishers generally feel more secure working with a subject that has proved its worth, rather than a groundbreaking (no pun intended) idea that is an unknown.

When you sell yourself as a writer, you are selling your experience. Spend hours, if not days, developing a résumé on your background in the field that you wish to write in. If you've been gardening for 10 years, say so. When you have won awards for your flowers or vegetables, list them on your résumé. Include classes that you have attended or taught. Show publishers that you are an authority on gardening. If you do this, you can almost count on getting a contract offer.

Do you like to travel? Would you like to make your trips tax-deductible and get paid for traveling? Become a travel writer. It helps if you are also a competent photographer. If you can deliver a manuscript with photos of a recent trip to a magazine, the editors may buy it. You don't have to be Mark Twain to make it as a writer. Write about what you know and love, and you probably will find success. Most of the work is in selling yourself, not necessarily your writing ability, to a publisher. If you are good at coming up with fresh ideas and describing your abilities, you most likely will make it as a writer of nonfiction work.

Work for Hire

If you are a writer who is willing to work for hire, you can pull in money from many sources. Nonprofit organizations are places to turn. Hospitals are other sources. Local businesses may hire you for a variety of assignments. Individuals might want you to write their résumés. If you are willing to write at will for customers, there is a broad market to work with. No one assignment is likely to pay outstanding rates, but if you save your pennies, they turn into dollars.

Many people despise written communication. Some of the highest-paid executives shrink at the thought of having to write a letter. Business owners often put off correspondence because it's not productive time. If you convince these businesspeople that you can improve their business with your writing skills, you may find that the keyboard is mightier than the sword of poverty. In other words, make your services known and watch your bank account grow.

Some ideas for business writing include the following: advertising copy, annual reports, letters, company policies, brochures, and so forth. Every growing business has a need for the written word. If you become known as a master wordsmith among the business community, you can reap rich rewards.

A big advantage to engaging in a writing career as a moonlighter is that all your production work can be performed at home.

You will need computer equipment, but not necessarily a state-of-the-art system. Word processing doesn't require a fast computer or even a large hard drive. Most equipment will produce good work. A laser printer is needed for the best presentations, but these once-expensive tools are not so expensive anymore.

Start-up costs for a writer are low if you don't count the expense of a computer, monitor, and printer. Even if you have to buy the equipment, you can shop the used market and set yourself up for well under $1,000. Considering the potential wealth involved with writing, this investment is well worth it.

PAINTERS AND SCULPTORS

Painters and sculptors are two types of people who can do well with sales stands and mail-order catalogs. Picasso probably never sold a painting by mail order or over the Internet, but today's painters have this opportunity. The money made from individual sales normally is not extravagant, but it all adds up. Custom, signature-series work can bring large sums of cash. Don't make the mistake of thinking that your art is only good in your eyes. Show it to the public and see what they think. You may be surprised.

About the only thing I can paint well is a fence or a house. I'm no artist when a brush is put in my hand. Writing and photography are my creative areas of endeavor. My wife, Kimberley, however, is an outstanding artist with a brush and paints. Her sculpting work is also good enough to attract plenty of attention. I've often tried to get Kimberley to showcase and sell her work. Most of my efforts have failed. She's convinced that if she turns her hobby into a profession, she will lose her interest in the work. Maybe this is true, I don't know. What I do know is that many people have offered hefty sums of money for her work.

If you are a painter or a sculptor, many cash-flow opportunities certainly are waiting for you. I believe that there are two distinct types of artists in these areas: people who paint and make sculptures for money, and others whose creative souls couldn't care less about cashing in on their art. Can you see painting hundreds of pictures to fill the suites of a hotel? Many artists would jump at this chance. Others, such as Kimberley, turn up their noses at the commercial smell of such a job.

Hotels and motels are good targets for the sale of photographs and paintings. Banks and other commercial institutions fall into this category. Are you willing to do production work to fill the walls of commercial spaces with pictures of a pleasant, if not original, nature? If you are, there is some money to be made.

Selling in bulk to major corporations is not the only way to make money from your art. Many local businesses, such as banks and restaurants, allow artists to display their work in a confined area that feels like a gallery. This can attract the attention of people who might commission you to produce custom pieces. If you undertake creating a signature series, you might make more money than you ever imagined possible from your art.

A Signature Series

Let me give you an example of how a signature series might work. Covered bridges have long been a source of interest and have been in the vernacular since the bestselling novel was published. Vermont has a number of beautiful covered bridges in it. There are others in the New England area. Suppose you decided to paint each and every covered bridge in Vermont and offer a limited edition of the prints. If you signed and numbered each print, the value would typically be much higher than if you simply sold an individual painting of the bridge. This is strong marketing strategy. Who would buy your prints? How about the businesses in Vermont? Hey, that's a good guess.

You don't have to tie a signature series to a particular locale. Maybe you will concentrate on painting wolves or whales. Both of these subjects have loyal followers. You could sell your prints of these creatures on a large level. Advertising in national magazines would be one way to cash in. Television commercials would be another. With signed and numbered prints, you could command handsome prices for your wildlife work. Before you know it, you could be a household name and could be pulling in more money than you would have imagined.

Sculptors of endangered wildlife can elicit a lot of attention. As a business owner, you can use all the free publicity that you can get. If you were to show your work on major news channels and in newspapers, you would quickly build a name for yourself. Your sculptures could become an enviable commodity if they are released in limited quantities, signed, and numbered.

Many artists have trouble coming to terms with the commercial value of what they do out of passion. If you want to be like Kimberley and keep your art to yourself, that is your privilege. However, so many people in this world will pay fair prices for your work that it wouldn't hurt too much to sell some of it. Pick a niche for yourself and keep it private, but turn the rest of your ability into a moonlighting adventure.

ARTS AND CRAFTS

When we speak of arts and crafts, we are opening the door to a vast opportunity. A few things you can make to sell include:

- Picnic tables
- Wishing wells
- Ceramics
- Baskets
- Wreaths
- Quilts

- Dream catchers
- Woodworking of all kinds
- Sewing of all types

Woodworkers, people who sew quilts, and dozens of other crafts-people come to mind. Almost anything that you enjoy doing around the house might fit into this category. And arts and crafts are popular among buyers and sellers. Baskets, weather vanes, stone paintings, wind chimes, and so much more can fall into this group of moneymaking ideas. Where do you fit in?

What do you like to do? How often do you visit gift shops? Kimberley and I were in a gift shop not long ago. I had been there with my parents when they came up for a visit, and there was something that I wanted to show Kimberley. I know, as a businessperson, how important it is to check out the competition and to stay abreast of current trends.

The gift shop, which is somewhat famous in Maine, was offering small portions of slate with paintings applied to the stone. One piece had a pair of puffins painted on the stone. It was a small piece with a big price tag. The going price for the puffins painted on a piece of scrap slate was $65. I knew what the price was, but Kimberley didn't. After showing her the piece, I asked her how long it would take her to paint it. She said that she could do it in less than 30 minutes. There you go, $130 dollars an hour from painting puffins on rock if you have a market. If the work is on consignment, as the samples I showed her probably are, you might get only half of the money. Still, $65 an hour is not a bad way to spend your spare time.

Painters are not the only ones who can command, and get, high prices for their work. My father is a woodworker. He does it only as a hobby. Try as I have, I can't convince him to sell what he makes. Friends that I have around this area, however, have listened to me, and they are turning some nice profits. Everything from picnic tables to wishing wells are bringing in big bucks for the people who devote their spare time to working with wood.

Ceramics, baskets, wreaths, quilts, dream catchers, and a host of other items sell like crazy. The only hard part is finding and meeting your market. Fortunately, this is not so difficult as most people believe. The biggest obstacle that you may have to overcome is learning that what you do as a hobby is a profitable venture. People will pay high prices for what you consider fun. This is what makes moonlighting so great. You can do what you enjoy and get paid for it. There is some work involved, such as advertising and filling orders, but the rest of it is fun.

When you want to make your moonlighting money working on crafts, you have dozens of choices. First, let's talk about how you sell what you make. Flea markets are outlets. Putting your work on consignment in specialty shops can work well, but you have to sell at discounted prices to the retailers who display your work. This is only fair, for the store owners are paying the rent, utilities, advertising, and labor required to sell your goods. If you are willing to invest some money in mail-order ads and a picture catalog, you can keep all the profits for yourself. Selling crafts by mail is big business. You might even pick up major mail-order sellers who will buy in bulk from you. While you won't make as much money on a per-piece price, you will make up for it in quantity sales.

Marketing, advertising, and fulfillment are often the most costly and most frustrating part of doing business. This is true of most businesses, and applies to the sale of crafts. If you can become associated with an outfit that is already established in the field, you can concentrate your efforts on the artistic work and allow the business operators to handle the less-desirable work. You work for less, but you avoid the hassles. This is not a bad approach to take as a moonlighter.

A fairly new outlet for sales is the Internet. If you set up your own Web page on the Internet, you can use it to sell your wares.

The exposure you get could reach millions of people. Think about this. Millions of people having access to your Web page could make you rich beyond your wildest dreams. Don't rule out any outlet for what you do as a moonlighter. As our world changes, we must change with it. Now let's get to the nitty-gritty of what some of your craft-making options are.

Woodworking

Woodworking is a popular hobby and a lucrative moonlighting business. You can build birdhouses, wishing wells, furniture, cabinets, model trains, or anything else you enjoy doing. There is a market for all types of wood products. Decoys made of wood command high prices, as do personalized name plaques. You could set up a stand at a busy place and customize desk nameplates, door plaques, and similar signage while your customers wait. People love to watch craftspeople at work, so doing your job right at your sales booth is a good idea.

Sewing

Sewing is something that people used to do at home. These days, most people buy what they need rather than make it. If you like to sew, you can create specialty items that will sell well. Quilts are always good sellers, and they bring big dollars to the table. Aprons are another nice market that can pay off, especially if you customize them with a slogan or a customer's name.

An area of sewing that can be very profitable is the custom sewing of wedding dresses. If you can become known for your quality work in this field, you can make a lot of money with your sewing machine. Handmade dolls are another good area to invest your sewing time in. Making drapes and curtains is another way to moonlight.

Depending on your interests, you may want to open your own sewing shop for alterations. Not only can you attract individual customers, you may be able to work out arrangements with clothing stores to do their alteration work as a pieceworker. There is always a need for people who are handy with needle and thread.

Ceramics

Ceramics can produce good part-time income. If you have a place to display what you make, a lot of people may become interested in your work. Taking your items to flea markets, malls, or other places where you can exhibit them is a good idea. You might even decide to create a catalog and sell your pieces by mail. If you have a kiln, you can cook up some homemade money pretty quickly.

Other Options

Other craft options are numerous. Needlepoint, knitting, and crocheting can help you make a profit when working from home. Your goods can be sold by mail, on consignment, or at exhibits. Making baskets is one way to generate moonlighting money at home. Taking your baskets and creating dried-flower arrangements is another way. If you want to work the circuit of fairs and events, you might invest in some airbrush equipment and paint T-shirts. For that matter, tie-dyeing T-shirts can make your cash register ring.

People who make rugs often do very well financially. Making wreaths can mean big money, especially during the holiday seasons. Carving logs into statues with a chain saw is not a common hobby, but some people make a lot of money from doing just this. Basically, anything that you enjoy doing can be turned into a money-making venture.

6

COMPUTER-GENERATED CASH

Computers are becoming as common in homes as televisions are. In a few more years, almost every home may have a computer in it. If you own a home computer, you can put it to work in your moonlighting business. As a matter of fact, you can make it your moonlighting business. Making money with your home computer offers a variety of perks. One of the best is that your work is produced at home.

Many moonlighters say that they work from home. Is there a difference between working from home and working at home? Absolutely. Working at home means that you perform your duties within the confines of your house. Saying that you work from home can mean simply that you use your home as an office. Your primary work function may be performed at any number of places. This is a significant difference.

Most moonlighting ventures allow you to work from home. Many of them, however, do not give you the freedom to work at home. Computers do give you the ultimate freedom of working at home, at your own pace, and at your own choice of hours. If you want to work at 2 A.M. you can. This is another big advantage to a work-at-home selection of moonlighting choices.

Many forms of moonlighting can be performed at unusual hours of the day and night. Some types of work require contact with people, and these choices dictate a more regimented set of work hours. When you are working with your computer, there is no limit to when you work. This all adds up to more opportunity to make extra money.

You can use your computer as a high-tech typewriter, or you can turn it into a powerful design tool. It's up to you. So many hardware and software options are available to choose from that anyone interested in computers can find plenty to do. Of course, not everyone has a computer. If you fall into this category, you may have to do a little shopping before you advertise your new computing services.

A PRIMER

In case you are not familiar with computers, let me give you a brief primer on what to look for and what to look out for when you buy one. Computer questions to consider are:

- How fast does my computer need to be?
- Do I want an IBM or a Macintosh format?
- What size hard drive do I need?
- Should I get a desktop, laptop, or notebook computer?
- Will I be working much with graphics?
- What size monitor do I need?
- Is a laser printer right for me?
- Do I need a color printer?
- Should I buy an internal or external modem?

Computer prices seem to drop each day. New technology and equipment is introduced on a regular basis. When this happens, equipment that was top-of-the-line a week ago is yesterday's news, so its price drops.

This is not a computer book, and we are not going to dig into each and every megabyte of details on computers. Basically, you have two choices in types of computers: IBM-compatible computers are used most often in general business applications. Macintosh computers are touted for being user-friendly and good with graphics. Before you decide which format you will use, you should visit local computer stores and get some free demonstrations.

I've never owned anything but IBM formats, so I can't give you firsthand reports on the capabilities of a Macintosh. I know that many artists use these computers for desktop publishing and related graphics. While IBM formats and Macintosh formats are not compatible, software is available for each type of computer that will do almost anything you would ever want to do on a computer.

After you decide which type of computer you want, IBM or Macintosh, you have a number of other decisions to make. How fast does your computer need to be? What is the smallest hard drive you are willing to work with? Should you buy a desktop, laptop, or notebook model? What type of printer and monitor will you buy? Answers to these questions vary, depending on individual needs.

You don't need a fast computer to perform word-processing work. It's not even mandatory to have a hard drive for this type of work. If you plan to produce a lot of graphics, however, you need speed and a high-capacity hard drive. People who do desktop publishing and page layouts find monitors that let them see an entire page all at once an advantage. Most users don't need to spend the large amount of money required to buy a full-page monitor. Laser printers give the best quality, but they are also expensive. To buy a laser printer that prints in color is more expensive. Ink-jet printers can be good compromises.

We don't have the space here to present a complete rundown of what you should buy and how much it may cost. But we can bounce around a few ideas. If your major interest is word processing, you can buy a used computer setup that includes a monitor and a printer for less than $600. New systems are available for less than $1,000.

If your work is going to be heavily oriented toward graphics, you should spend more money to get a faster, newer machine. A reasonable starting point is probably around $1,500. In general terms, you can set yourself up to do almost anything for less than $2,000. It's also easy to spend five times that amount if you want the best of everything. You will have to set your own budget and identify your personal needs. Once you have your system, you're ready to start making money. How are you going to do this? Some ways to make money with a computer are:

- Typing
- Data entry
- Writing
- Résumés
- Transcription work
- Term papers for students
- Annual reports
- Brochures
- Catalogs
- Desktop publishing
- Menus
- Logos
- Business cards
- Newsletters
- Bookkeeping
- Computer-aided drawing (CAD) work

- Advertising designs
- Research work

A Simple Typing Business

A simple typing business can turn your spare time into spare cash. You don't have to own expensive equipment or possess unusual skills to make money as a freelance typist. Many people either don't have the equipment, skills, or patience to do their own typing. This is good for the home-based typist.

What types of documents will people ask you to prepare? Résumés are a common request. In my area, people get about $30 to type up a preprepared résumé. When a custom résumé is wanted, the price jumps to well over $50. Wills are not so uncommon as you might think. General correspondence is sometimes requested. If you get hooked up with the right professionals, you can transcribe their recorded tapes into written words. There is very good money in this, and many doctors, lawyers, and similar professionals engage the services of outside freelancers for transcription work. If you can perform transcription work, you can build a full-time business very quickly. Word travels fast in professional circles. Once you demonstrate your ability, you are sure to receive some word-of-mouth referral business.

Students are a customer base that you might not think of. I know freelancers who make serious money working with college students. By typing term papers for the students, the freelancers stay busy and profitable. Getting student business is easy. Post a notice in various school locations and watch the work roll in.

Annual reports for businesses is another lucrative field. Some freelancers earn thousands of dollars doing just one report. It can be time-consuming, but the compensation is good. You might also make money transcribing the minutes of meetings for businesses. There is a constant need in business for paperwork, so if you make business owners aware of your services, you should see an upward growth trend.

BROCHURES AND CATALOGS

Businesses pay handsome prices to the people who prepare their brochures and catalogs. If you are set up with desktop publishing equipment and know how to use it, you can make major money in this field. For a simple trifold brochure, the type that you pick up in tourist stops, you may make anywhere from $500 to $1,000, and sometimes more.

Being a good photographer can be an advantage when you are producing brochures and catalogs, for much of the work depends on photographs. If you are willing to offer customers a complete package deal, one in which you create the brochure, have it printed, and deliver it, you can make even more money. Why will you make more? Let me explain.

If you go to a business owner and offer to design and create a master copy of a brochure, price is bound to come up in the conversation. If you ask for $750, the business owner may wince in pain. But suppose you told the customer that you could produce a turnkey job and that each brochure would cost only three cents. This sounds easier to swallow, doesn't it? By taking on the entire job, you spread out your profit and distribute it in a way that is not so shocking. It works.

You can divide your cost to create a master copy by a hypothetical number of prints and provide a customer with a low per-piece price. If you can sell the business owner a volume of copies, you might be able to incorporate your design work with the cost of a print run and still keep the price per piece in pennies. Depending on what you are doing, the price might range from less than a nickel to more than a quarter, but when you give your prices based on pocket change, customers don't usually feel overwhelmed.

MENUS

Have you ever considered how many restaurants are in your local area? Places that serve food and drink need menus. Could you create these menus? Of course you could. And you could probably convince managers and owners of restaurants that your customized menus would be good for business. Think about it. You go out to dinner and read the menu. Ask the waitperson to leave it. Pull out your pencil and mark it up with proposed changes. Before you leave, ask to speak to the manager. Pitch your idea and you might leave with a full stomach and a new account as a menu planner.

OTHER BUSINESS IDEAS

Other business ideas include designing logos, creating company letterheads, laying out business cards, and typesetting magnetic signs. Real estate salespeople often are good prospects for typing services. You might be able to obtain contracts to produce brochures, newspaper columns, or newsletters for brokerages and agents. A number of companies offer this type of service to the real estate industry, but there is always room for one more.

Many people who start off providing typing services expand their sales with other services. You might become a dealer for a rubber-stamp company. Another idea is to become a sales outlet for companies that produce magnetic signs. The potential goes on and on. Become a notary public. Offer to fax documents for a fee. If you have a copy machine, sell copies. Your customers are usually business-oriented, so stock up on some business-related supplies that you can sell at a markup.

Specialized Word-Processing Services

Once you get beyond basic typing, you reach a level of specialized word-processing services. Let's say that your full-time job has made you experienced with legal documents. You could offer your services to lawyers as a legal secretary or in some related capacity. If you are good with numbers, an accounting firm might use your services.

Writers often seek assistance from freelance editors, especially if the writers have not yet been published. This type of writer wants someone to edit and critique his or her work before it is submitted to a potential publisher. If you possess good grammar skills, you can fill this need.

Ghostwriting can be a lucrative moonlighting proposition. If you are good with written communication and a keyboard, you can become a team player for someone who wishes to write a book. Let the author dictate notes and passages while you transcribe them from tapes. This type of work normally falls into the hands of established, published writers, but this is not to say that you can't get a piece of the action.

Look at your personal skills. Where do they place you in the business world? Try to match the services you offer the public to your strengths. In doing this, you can present yourself as something of an expert and command higher rates. There is quite a lot that you can do with a simple computer system and some word-processing software.

Computer-Aided Drawing (cad) Programs

Computer-aided drawing (CAD) programs have made it possible for people who are not good with a pencil and paper to draw detailed plans of almost anything. You can make money in many ways with CAD work. But you will need a fast computer that has a hefty hard drive. You should also have a plotter and a printer. This type of setup can be expensive, but the payback comes quickly once you attract customers.

One of the best opportunities that I know of for CAD operators is drawing house plans and blueprints for remodeling projects. Your customers may be homeowners, prospective homeowners, remodelers, builders, or even lumber suppliers. You don't have to be a licensed architect to take advantage of the need for detailed, scaled drawings in the construction and remodeling trades.

Don't attempt to draw in structural aspects of a set of plans unless you are working with a rough sketch from a qualified designer. However, don't hesitate to draw scaled floor plans, kitchen cabinet layouts, landscaping plans, and other nonstructural drawings. The money here can be very, very good. Let me give you a few hints on how to break into the market.

Many people dream of building their own home or of remodeling the home that they live in. Before these people can realize their dreams, someone must put a basic plan on paper. This plan can be created with pen and paper, but a CAD system allows for a much better perspective. You can even draw three-dimensional images, so that it's possible to get a more complete view of what a project will look like. You can advertise and reach consumers directly, but this tends to be expensive in relation to the number of jobs you are likely to get.

Better sources of business that are not so expensive to reach are lumberyards, builders, and remodelers. All these people provide their customers with drawings from time to time. If you can make a contractor look extremely professional by providing a CAD kitchen design, you can expect to be paid for it, and probably pretty well. Network with people in the industry and make yourself known as a CAD operator for hire.

As a home builder, I've paid drafting companies close to $1,000 for a set of house plans. These included some architectural information, so they cost more than a basic floor plan. But you can still make hundreds of dollars for each job you do. If you hook up with the right contractors and suppliers, you may very well make more money moonlighting than you do at your regular job. It helps if you possess some basic knowledge of construction and design principles, but you are not required to. After all, it's your creative, and accurate, drawings that people are paying for.

AUTOMATED ESTIMATING PROGRAMS

Automated estimating programs have made it easy for big-league contractors to figure out what materials and how much labor they will need to do a job. When a contractor has the right estimating equipment, it's possible to pinpoint labor and material much more effectively than doing a takeoff by hand would allow. Fortunately for you, many contractors are not equipped with this sophisticated equipment. Here is yet another opportunity for you. And if you are already dealing with contractors on CAD work, this is an easy add-on that will put extra money in your pocket.

Many professional estimating programs are available to contractors. They are designed for plumbers, electricians, general contractors, and other types of related professions. A vast group of contractors, however, don't have access to these high-tech systems. In some cases the systems cost too much for contractors to justify purchasing them. Sometimes contractors would rather be building and plumbing than learning how to use computer software. Regardless of the reasons, a huge number of contractors don't have automated estimating equipment. If you've got it, there is a strong market for you to pursue.

The contractor market is easy to go after. All you have to do is look in the telephone book under various contracting categories. Prospects are abundant. You don't have to know much about plumbing or building or electrical work to do automated estimating. You plug in some numbers, which your customers should be willing to supply, run a pen around the lines of blueprints, and presto!, you have an estimate.

Don't expect to get rich from any one job when you are doing automated estimating. But your customers are likely to keep coming back for more work, and you also can sell them on other services. There aren't a lot of people providing this service, so it is a good one to break into.

COMPUTERIZED BOOKKEEPING

Computerized bookkeeping is another good market for you to consider. With the right software, you don't have to do much of anything, except enter information provided to you by your customers. The most difficult part of this job is usually in getting your customers to provide timely, organized entry information to you.

Think about all the small businesses that are in your area. Many of them have fewer than five employees. But every one of them needs some form of bookkeeping. When a small company has employees, the need for solid bookkeeping escalates. This is your opening.

If you check telephone directories, you will find bookkeeping and payroll services offered by others. Don't let this spook you. The bigger companies usually are going after bigger clients than your niche market will be. If you concentrate on companies that have fewer than ten employees, you will greatly reduce the amount of competition that you must contend with.

Big bookkeeping and payroll services like large accounts. If they hook corporations with 75 employees, their profit per contact goes up. You will need more clients to fill out your roster, but you can get them. As one small business to another, you can build a certain rapport. Plus, many big companies don't want to deal with extremely small businesses. You can pick up where they leave off and build a nice future for yourself.

Call, write, or visit small businesses in your area. Show them examples of what you are capable of. For example, show them mock-ups of payroll records, expenses, income, financial statements, inventory control, and so forth. Pitch them on how having you perform these services will free them up to do what they do best. Many small-time business owners will jump on this one. Go on to express how accurate and organized record keeping can be invaluable in a tax audit. This can scare a prospect into agreeing to your terms. With the right sales pitch, you can get more business than you will have time to tend to.

CAMERA-READY ADVERTISEMENTS

Businesses that advertise in newspapers and magazines need camera-ready artwork. If your computer is equipped with a scanner, clip art, and a graphics program, you can pull in some money by helping businesses prepare their advertising. A potential drawback to this is that deadlines must sometimes be met, so you may have to work fast and hard. Overall though, the work usually is calm and profitable.

If you have a background in advertising, you can offer your services as a consultant. Otherwise, just agree to take the rough drafts that business owners provide you and turn them into camera-ready advertisements. You might get clients from small businesses or larger ones. Catching the attention of business owners can be accomplished with your own ads. If owners call you, it means that they were motivated to act on your ad. This is good credibility for your ability to design and create working advertisements for them.

Pay Up

Many businesses suffer with bad credit accounts. Customers who don't pay their bills can put a company into deep financial trouble. The cost of turning a bad account over to a collection agency or attorney can be quite steep. You can offer business owners an alternative. Tell them that you will prepare and send collection notices for them. Offer this service on either a flat-rate, per-letter, or commission basis. Most collection agencies and attorneys work on a commission basis. You might do better by getting a flat rate for each collection letter you mail. Almost any service business has its share of bad debts to collect, so you might just hit it right and get rich in this field.

Before you start sending out mail or making telephone calls to collect money for business owners, it would be wise to talk to your attorney. Find out when you can call people and what you can say. There usually are laws that prohibit telephone calls for credit collection at certain times of the day or night. Have your attorney draw up a few fill-in-the-blank collection letters that you can use as models. You will pay a little for this service, but it should keep you on the right side of the law.

RESEARCH

A computer with the right connections is a powerful research tool. It's possible that you could use your computer to perform research services for customers. Students are one possibility to work with. Lawyers might pay you to research various matters for them. Business owners may pay you to provide a variety of research services. The demand for this type of work is not usually high, but it can be enough to add to your part-time earnings from other computer-related work.

Computers are changing quickly, and so are the moneymaking opportunities that go hand in hand with them. If computers are your idea of fun, you can make money moonlighting while doing what you enjoy. There is always a demand for quality help in the business world. When you have the right skills and equipment, you can find plenty of work. Crank up your computer, and watch your bank account grow.

7
KIDS' STUFF

hildren are our future, and they can be your profit center. The
money made on products and services aimed at parents is aston-
ishing. Parents buy everything from stuffed animals to fancy
shoes and hair ties. I should know; I have two children and spend
more money on them than I care to count. Whether you have children or not, this is one market that is very lucrative. It doesn't matter if you are running a day-care facility, offering diaper services,
or making toys for tots: a lot of money can be made.

Prior to having children, I never fully appreciated how much
money parents spend on their youngsters. The spending starts
before birth and probably never ends. No doubt, entrepreneurs can
do very well working within the markets aimed at children and
parents.

What kinds of products and services do parents pay for? The
market is vast. Following are ways to cash in on kid stuff:

- Writing letters to children on a subscription basis
- Offering holiday mailings
- Planning parties
- Running a secondhand clothing outlet

- Building dollhouses
- Selling bedtime stories on cassette tapes
- Offering pet rentals
- Creating wooden toys
- Sewing keepsake blankets
- Making rocking horses
- Offering a diaper service
- Providing day-care facilities
- Giving pony rides
- Playing a clown for hire
- Selling ice cream
- Offering security suggestions and services to parents

Clothes, blankets, furniture, day care, and toys only begin to mark the territory. This is truly a field where you can start with one or two items or services and grow into a major business.

Where should you start? You must take a look at yourself and your goals to decide what portion of the market to take advantage of. The overall market is far too large to conquer all of it. One or two specialties will get your business into high gear.

MONEY FROM MAIL

Money from mail is very possible when you enter the market of children. Children love to receive letters and packages in the mail. Not all children have enough relatives to satisfy their desire for mail. Going to the mailbox to see if anything is there for you can be a big thrill for a child. My grandfather got me hooked on watching for the mail delivery.

More than 30 years have passed since I used to sit on the porch with my grandfather, hoping there would be something for me, and mail delivery is still a major interest in my day. Is this because my grandfather ingrained it in me? Maybe. For whatever reason, I still love to check the mailbox. My daughter shares my enthusiasm. From what I've read and heard, other children also look forward to receiving mail. This is your opportunity for a moonlighting service.

You can advertise your services in parenting magazines to obtain fast responses. Ads in other areas, such as newspapers, also can work. Renting a mailing list of people who have young children also can get you off to a fast start. I would opt for the magazine ads and the mailing lists. Newspapers probably won't pull in a lot of business.

What is it that you are doing? You are writing letters to children on a regular basis. Sell your services by subscription. Charge a certain amount to send a letter to a child once a month. Step up the frequency of the correspondence and charge more.

Children probably don't want to hear from someone they don't know. Getting a letter from Roger Woodson probably will not impress many children. Come up with some catchy names to work with. For example, a child might receive a letter one time from Hilda the Hippo and then get a letter from Earl the Elephant. Create logos, art, and stationery for each of your communication characters. Send a sample to parents on request. Once they see your diversity, they may be very prone to signing up for many mailings.

You also can offer theme mailings. A list of dinosaurs might be appropriate. Coming up with a group of names for space aliens might trigger a response. So many theme characters are being offered to the public today that you won't have to think too hard to find areas that interest you. Put together a group of people who fit the mold of various television shows. You don't have to copy the shows to make a strong sales approach. Whether your made-up characters resemble a purple dinosaur, a large yellow bird with long legs, or some weird turtles, you can cash in on the craze. If you have children, you probably know the types of characters I'm talking about. On the chance that you don't have young children, tune into the television channels that feature shows for children. You can get a lot of ideas this way.

Holidays are a special time. They are also good opportunities for you to earn some bonus money on your letter-writing subscriptions to children. And don't forget that many people now have fax machines and e-mail service available to them in their homes. These technologies expand your market even further.

How long has it been since the Easter Bunny wrote your child a letter? Did your son or daughter receive a response from the North Pole the past year? Did anyone ever send you or your children a special note for Halloween or Thanksgiving? When you key in on the holidays, you have a good chance to pick up extra money. Mail it, fax it, or e-mail it. People love this type of attention. If you have a good feel for what children like and can communicate with them on their level, you will own a growing business with very little overhead expense and a good profit potential.

Party Planning

Party planning and coordinating is a growing field in the children's market, particularly now that in many instances both parents work at demanding jobs. Sure, some people take their children to the Golden Arches for a birthday party, but those parents are seeking alternatives. Having 12 wild children crashing through your home is a sobering and scary experience. Many parents are opting for birthday parties away from home. The parties are being held at amusement parks, restaurants, campgrounds, and many other places. You can get a piece of this action by taking care of all the details. Some work is involved, but it's not unreasonable when compared with the rates that you can charge.

Two years ago, I paid to hold my daughter's birthday party at a facility that caters to private parties. The building was filled with children's games. It was like a miniature amusement park. The building also contained tables and chairs. Cake and ice cream, along with drinks, were served by the staff, but my wife and I had to provide the food, plates, and disposable utensils. Operating a place like this could be profitable in a highly populated area. The one we used is in rural Maine, and it's still in business.

You don't have to convert your basement into a party playhouse. It's entirely possible to make good money just acting as a broker of sorts. All you do is make arrangements for parents. It is not your responsibility to provide a physical location for a party on your premises. Instead, you line up a party at one of any potential party sites.

Your job might require arranging for a room, completing a mailing to everyone on a guest list, seeing that food is catered, and so on. You might even contact people on the invitation list to suggest particular presents for the birthday child. You can take this type of service business to any level.

SECONDHAND CLOTHING

At one time, wearing hand-me-downs was frowned on, but this no longer is the case. Check your local telephone book. You probably will find several secondhand clothing stores listed. How many of them cater to children? Clothes are not the only secondhand items that can be recycled to new customers. Toys, strollers, cribs, and a wide array of other items all fit the bill for a secondhand store.

If you want to set up a retail business, you may need to rent retail space. Rent can be quite expensive. On the other hand, if you have a garage or basement, you might be able to operate your new business from home. It depends on how convenient your home is to customers and what the zoning laws in your area are. In any event, you can make major money for used things worn and needed by children.

Parents will come to your shop to sell you some items and buy other items while they are in the store. Flea markets offer great values for you to buy and resell. Ads in local newspapers will get your telephone ringing with people who want to sell you everything from baby monitors to playground slides. If you buy smart, buy cheap, and sell high, you will operate a profitable business. The second-hand market is growing and offering outstanding potential to full-time workers and moonlighters.

DOLLHOUSES

What little girl doesn't want a fancy dollhouse at some time in her life? It's inevitable that little girls fall in love with dollhouses somewhere along their way to maturity. The truth is, some middle-aged women are still intrigued with nice dollhouses. Here you have a number of options. If you are handy, you can build dollhouses to sell. You can even custom build them to the specifications of parents. Doing this makes the price soar, so give it some thought.

When it comes to creating dollhouses to sell, you can choose to build them by hand, put together kits, or modify existing, commercial dollhouses. Building dollhouses from scratch is not a particularly difficult job for a person who is comfortable with woodworking. If you don't know a router from a jigsaw, however, maybe you had better look for some alternative to building miniature homes.

The time and effort that can be invested in building a top-quality dollhouse deserves a high dollar. If your dollhouses are extraordinary, you probably can command, and get, mind-boggling money for them. But if you prefer to work fast and for a little less money on each sale, you have two options.

Have you ever had to put together a bicycle? When was the last time that you constructed a Fort Apache or some other multi-piece toy? Many parents hate the idea of assembling anything. Here is your opportunity as a moonlighter. Dollhouses are sold in kit form. If you buy the kits, you don't have to make all the fancy cuts on the wood. All you have to do is put the kit together. Some folks find this process a form of therapy. Imagine, receiving therapy and getting paid for it at the same time. What could be better?

Buy a variety of dollhouse kits and put them together. Once they are completed, you can sell them for hefty profits. Parents love to buy preassembled units. Add some wiring and battery-operated lights, and your price shoots up considerably. Take the time to wallpaper some of the walls and add several other key decorative features, such as crown molding, and the price continues to climb. Even though you are selling kit homes, your special handiwork has made them unique, so they are worth much more to many parents.

If you are all thumbs when it comes to assembly work, buy pre-constructed houses and add decorative touches. Paint, wallpaper, furniture, and similar add-ons make the value go up. If you are really good at this, you can offer the dollhouses as a signature series. They can be considered family heirlooms, to be passed down to future generations. You can imagine what this will do for the value of a product.

Selling dollhouses can be accomplished in a number of ways. You can advertise and sell them directly on a local level. Advertise in national magazines and make a mail-order fortune. Put your finished homes on consignment in toy stores and gift shops. Set up a booth in a mall and watch the money roll in. Depending on how much you charge for your product, it can be very helpful to be established as a credit-card merchant. First-class dollhouses can sell for hundreds of dollars.

RECORDING STORIES

Do you have a soothing voice? If you do, you can record bedtime stories for children and sell the tapes. Some cost is involved in making the master tapes and duplicating them, but the profit potential for this type of work is fantastic. Good stories are always a favorite with children. If you have the type of voice that records well, you can make a career out of telling stories on tape.

The stories you record must be material that you create. Don't read books or tell the stories of others when making your recordings. Copyright laws protect the works of others, so make sure that all your stories are created in your own mind to avoid legal complications.

The last time I checked, I could get full use of a recording studio, complete with an engineer, for only $25 an hour. My reasons for looking into this had to do with seminars and tape sets. But the same rates would have applied to any kind of tapes. With a prepared script, I could have recorded for a full day and paid only $200 for the master tapes. If each story lasted 15 minutes, I could have gotten 32 stories on tape for the low price of $200.

Duplicating the tapes is easy. The price for this depends on how many tapes you are duplicating at once. Even in small quantities, I could have gotten duplicates for less than $1 apiece. Let's assume that each tape has four 15-minute stories on it. These tapes probably would sell quickly at prices ranging from $4.95 to $9.95. Think of the profit to be made with this type of venture. It's out of this world, in terms of percentages.

Once you record the master tapes, you have nothing to do except sell and fill orders. Of course, you usually will have to add to your story collections. If you get parents to subscribe to your tape club, you can sell tapes to every customer every month. This really adds up in terms of profit. Your advertising money is capturing a repeat customer, which is the aim of every business owner.

It doesn't take a lot of money to sell bedtime tapes. If you have the creativity and voice to tell good stories, this could be your dream come true. It's a low-impact moonlighting venture that can be marketed locally, nationally, or on the Internet.

Piñatas

Piñatas are favorite attractions at birthday parties. Children love to take turns whacking the papier-mâché figures that contain candy and toys. I don't remember ever having a piñata at one of my birthday parties, but my daughter has had them for as long as I can remember. Other parties that my daughter has attended have had piñatas. There is a current trend to use this type of Mexican treat. And you can cash in on it by making piñatas.

Horses, unicorns, elephants, and a wide range of other animals can be the subjects of piñatas. These candy caches are made from simple papier-mâché and are easily constructed. If you enjoy working with your hands and have an eye toward children's products, piñatas may make sense for you. They can enhance the parties you arrange for children, if you decide to go that moonlighting route.

After you have created some prototype piñatas, you can sell them to gift stores and birthday stores. Parents will buy them directly from you. A mail-order business could be created with piñatas. You probably won't make a lot of money a month with your piñata business, but it can keep you in pocket money.

Pet Rentals

Have you ever heard of anyone renting pets? I can't say that I have, but it seems like a good idea. If you open your mind and think about it, you probably will agree that it makes sense. Children love pets. Children walk into a pet store and want everything they see. Once they have coerced their parents into a purchase, the children often may lose interest in their new pet, putting parents in a bad situation. What do you do with a pet that no longer is wanted? One solution is to give it back to the store where you bought it. This is why renting makes so much sense.

If you thought that you wanted to buy a motor home to vacation in, would you buy one right away or would you rent one to see if you really liked it? The smart money is on renting one. Our world is full of leases and rental plans. You can rent beds, televisions, refrigerators, bulldozers, and many other things. It's the old try-it-before-you-buy-it mentality. But it works. You can make it work for you by offering rental pets.

If you went door-to-door interviewing parents about pets that were wanted when they were purchased and ignored a few weeks later, I think you would find that a large percentage of pet purchases are regretted. As a parent, I know firsthand that this has been the case with my daughter from time to time. It's not just children that go through this. I've known adults who loved puppies but disliked dogs. Well, puppies become dogs, and this can create a serious problem for some people.

What would happen if you opened a pet-rental center? You could find that you have hit on the hottest idea of this decade. Think about it. If a child wants a hamster, one can be rented. Once the child and parents discover that hamsters bite, the animal could be returned to you. This is good for the people and the pet. The animal is not mistreated or ignored. You get it back to rent to someone else. The people who returned it might try a pet rat next. If they do, they will find that female rats tend to be very clean and cuddly with few biting episodes. To expand on this, let's look at some other examples.

Studies have shown that cats and dogs can be therapeutic for people. You could base part of your rental business on this positive note. Rent companion pets to people in their time of need. Take them back if the people tire of them. Have you always wondered if potbelly pigs are as good for pets as they are reported to be? If you could rent one for a month or two, you could find out.

To set up a pet-rental business, you need either a rural home with facilities for animals or an in-town retail space where you can house everything from snakes and dogs to parrots and pigs. To the best of my knowledge, this is an untested business, but I can see huge potential in it, especially if you add some spin-off profits.

What do I mean by spin-off profits? Don't just rent pets, sell them. You will be in competition with other pet stores, but I doubt if any of your competitors will let a buyer rent to own. In addition to renting and selling pets, you can stock a variety of pet supplies to sell. If you have the room, you can take in animals as a pet motel. Boarding animals is another lucrative field, and it is a natural extension of this type of business. Be advised, however, that most areas require licenses to deal in animals and to board them.

The start-up cost for a pet business can be steep. Don't attempt this type of business unless you are willing to invest money in both the animals and their habitats. It's only my opinion, but I think that someone who undertakes this business properly could make a large sum of money and perhaps sell franchise rights at a later date.

WOODEN TOYS

Wooden toys for children are so popular that entire books have been written about making them. You can open a book or magazine and find plenty of ideas and plans for wooden toys. These items range from simple blocks to jigsaw puzzles. Beds for baby dolls attract a lot of attention. Pull toys are always popular. If you are into woodworking, you can turn your shop into something of a Santa's workshop by making wooden toys for tots. These items can be sold through mail-order ads, at local events, and by general advertising. If you sign and number the pieces in limited editions, their value can escalate.

Keepsake Blankets

Keepsake blankets are favorites for children and parents. Most children have some type of blanket that they consider their security blanket. Did it start with Linus? I don't know if the Peanuts series had anything to do with the popularity of special security blankets or not, but I do know that you can make good money selling specialized blankets to parents.

My parents bought a handmade blanket for my daughter when she was born. They subsequently bought a second, identical, blanket from the same person. The extra blanket serves as a backup and standby blanket when "Bubbie" is being washed. After eight years, the original Bubbie is hanging tough, and the backup blanket is never far away. My daughter does not depend on her blanket, but she continues to love it.

Getting into the custom blanket business could make your spare time much more profitable. If you enjoy sewing, you can make a variety of blankets to sell. I would make them in limited editions, so that they would be worth more. Depending on your marketing plan, you could customize the blankets with a child's name or favorite character or scene. The potential is very good.

Rocking Horses

Rocking horses are traditional gifts for children. You can go to a toy store and buy a commercial rocking horse, but it's not the same as getting a custom-crafted steed for your son or daughter. Woodworkers can set up to mass-produce rocking horses in their basements or garages. If you want to sell unique rocking horses, you can fill the juvenile market and meet the collector market. Yes, people do collect rare and unusual rocking horses. You probably won't get rich from standard sales, but you can make a good return on your time when you make and sell rocking horses.

DIAPER SERVICE

Disposable diapers are here to stay, but some parents prefer using cloth diapers. If you don't mind doing the dirty work, you can offer a door-to-door diaper service. You drop off clean diapers and pick up dirty ones. Clean the soiled diapers and trade them for more dirty ones the next week. Once you establish a route, you can produce steady income. The business doesn't offer the highest profits possible for moonlighters, but it is a good way to maintain extra income. Another advantage to this type of job is that you can pick up and drop off after business hours.

DAY-CARE PROVIDER

Becoming a day-care provider is a big responsibility, but it can be extremely profitable. You may not consider day care as a viable alternative for a moonlighter, yet it can be. In some ways, offering day-care services at what would normally be considered odd hours can benefit you greatly. Most people think of day-care facilities that operate during the normal business day. This is, in fact, when most child-care places are busy. But there are other times when parents need someone responsible to watch over their children.

If you work a night shift at your regular job, you can offer day-care services in the traditional manner. But don't be discouraged if you are a regular day worker. Many parents do work night shifts, and you may be able to take care of their children for them while they work. With some luck, the children will be asleep for most of the time that you are watching them. The fact that you are offering after-hours day care means that you can charge more for your services.

Schoolteachers often seek part-time work during summer months, when school is out. Some of them paint houses, others work in restaurants and grocery stores. If you happen to be a teacher, you can provide summer day care for school-age children. Your credentials as a teacher will carry a lot of weight with parents, and summer programs fill up fast. This is a great opportunity for people who have their days free when school is closed.

Before and after school is a tough time for many parents. With school hours being what they are, it's hard for working parents to juggle domestic duties and professional requirements. There is a strong need for day care in the hours before and after school. If you are in a position to offer this type of care in a way that is convenient for both parents and children, you can cash in on some lucrative income.

Getting into day care can be expensive. You will probably need a license. You will have to either rent space for the care or remodel your home to accommodate children of various ages. A play area and playground normally will be needed. If you are taking care of small children, cribs and high chairs will be needed. You can start small and work your way up. This way, your first couple of customers pay for the added equipment you need to expand. Because you are living off the wages from your full-time job, you can use your earnings on the first few children to build a bigger, better business. Day-care service, even on a part-time basis, can reward you with comfortable bank deposits.

PONIES

Ponies and children go together like peanut butter and jelly. If you live in the country, or have access to a boarding facility, you can set yourself up to offer pony rides. You can do this either by getting contracts to work weekends at special events, such as fairs and carnivals, or by offering your services directly to the public. I know one person who does this very successfully in my area.

The person of whom I speak has a trailer for her pony. This allows her to take the pony to where the action is. It may be a clam festival one day, a fireworks display another day, and a town park the next. Where there are people, there can be profits waiting for the pony-ride person.

Getting into the pony-ride business can be more expensive than it's worth to some people. If you have facilities at home for ponies, you are way ahead of individuals who must board their animals. The expense and responsibility of keeping live animals is more than some people care to take on. If you like animals and want to mix in some profits with your pastime, however, pony rides are a good way to do it. As with just about any business, make sure that your insurance coverage is complete and adequate before you start calling in customers.

BE A CLOWN

If you like children, you can be a clown for hire. Showing up at birthday parties and other events as a humorous character is not only fun, it's profitable. The annual income may not be a lot when compared to other moonlighting ideas, but the hourly rates are strong. You don't need much to get started in this type of business. Once you are established, you can offer your services to general consumers and promoters of special events. You may find more work as a clown than you think you will.

I know an oral surgeon who enjoys doing magic tricks. This man goes to parties and events frequently as a magician. It's not that he needs the money, but he enjoys performing magic and watching people smile. Gee, I wonder if being a dentist has anything to do with his attraction for smiles? Whether you are a clown, a magician, or a walking french fry, you can find work at parties and special events.

Ice-Cream Vendor

Have you ever thought of becoming an ice-cream vendor? When you're out of work, children are out of school. You could jump into your ice-cream van and hit the streets before dark. Hearing the ding-ding-ding of an ice-cream truck always makes children want to run out and buy something. The start-up cost and overhead of this type of business may be more than you want to bite off, but it is a possible moneymaker.

Sell Consumer Safety

Parents are always concerned about the health and welfare of their children. Working parents don't have a lot of personal time to research the risks and dangers that their children face. You can make it easy for parents to put up protective walls around their children. No, you're not going to sell them bricks. It's information that you will be peddling.

If you have spare time on your hands, a computer, and a willingness to research materials, you can create your own gold mine.

Like pet rentals, this is a new idea that I don't believe has been tested or tried. But let me explain how I envision it will work.

You turn on your computer and tie into various data banks of information. Download all safety-related issues pertaining to children. Check libraries for back issues of magazines and similar sources of safety information. Compile all the facts and statistics into either a book or a newsletter. Advertise your condensed safety information in parenting magazines and on the Internet. Before you know it, parents will be lining up to obtain your user-friendly, direct information.

If you can provide parents fast access to a wide range of safety precautions and concerns, you are fulfilling a valuable service. Working parents don't have the time to read dozens of magazines and newspaper articles. Naturally, they are missing information that they should see. If you compile all the information and offer it to them in an organized manner, rich rewards may be in your future.

Children are a never-ending source of revenue for moonlighters. You don't have to come into contact with children to profit from them. But if you like dealing with children, plenty of opportunities are available for you to work with them. If I had to guess, I'd say the children of our world represent one of the largest-growing profit centers around. Give some thought to this. You might just find that your niche is in the nursery.

8

GENERAL SERVICES

When it comes to general services, there is no end to the possibilities for profit. Service providers continue to grow in number at enormous rates, and this is good for moonlighters like you. People today will pay for almost any type of service. You can make money changing lightbulbs for a person. Hey, I've done it, and thirty bucks a call to change lightbulbs ain't bad. Major money is available for service contractors, and you don't have to have a licensed skill to make big money in the field.

Everyone has areas of interest and knowledge in which they excel. If you can identify your strengths, you can use them to start your own service business. Most businesses of this type can be run from a home office. While you may, and probably will, have to go out to serve your clients, you won't need to rent a plush office downtown. There are options when customers come to you. In some cases, your work is conducted by telephone and fax, and you never have face-to-face meetings with your customers. Depending on the type of business that you choose, there is plenty of flexibility in when you work and what you do. This is ideal for a moonlighter.

What types of service businesses can you operate? This depends on you, but we will cover a variety of potential businesses for you to consider. As a teaser, let's talk about a few. Suppose you set yourself up as a business called Senior Services? You could check in on the elderly and infirm from time to time. Maybe you would bring their mail in or pick up groceries for them. Children of aging parents will pay to have someone keep an eye on their loved ones, especially if the children are not living in the immediate area.

Decorating a home can be the basis for your service business. If you have a flair for colors and patterns that work well together, you can sell your knowledge to homeowners who wish to remodel their homes. Or you could hang out your shingle as a meeting planner, a person who takes care of all the details of meetings for business clients. Making flower arrangements for local hospital gift shops is another idea worth considering. Training hunting dogs could be your calling. Well, enough of the tempting tidbits, let's jump right into the heart of things.

SENIOR SERVICES

I mentioned senior services just a moment ago, so let's run with this one. The idea behind this business is providing assistance to people who are unable to leave their homes easily. Samples of senior services include:

- Safety checks by telephone
- Personal visits
- Grocery deliveries
- In-home cooking
- Meal deliveries
- Administrating monthly expense payments

- Home maintenance
- Lawn maintenance

Your customers may be the people who are confined to their homes, but I see the market being their children. Children worry about their aging parents, and they want to take care of them. These days, many children live far from their parents, and you have an excellent opportunity to offer them a unique service.

Your services can include many options for customers to choose from. Maybe your job will be to call a person on the telephone every day to make sure that the person is OK. You might be required to make a personal visit, to see that the person is taking medication on schedule. Delivering groceries can be a big part of what you do. Having driveways plowed when it snows and walkways shoveled is another possibility. Keeping a person's grass cut and shrubbery trimmed can fit the bill. You might even find yourself reviewing the payment of monthly bills. There is no limit to what your participation in the care of an individual might be. This type of helpful work doesn't require a medical license. You are merely an on-call helper. Yet, you can make a lot of money providing this service.

Another market is people who are unable to care for themselves. They need help. Consider how fast surgery patients are sent home these days. This type of person can use your help in many ways, ranging from getting to the bathroom to fixing meals. So many families have both spouses working that if one of them is injured or recovering from surgery, an outsider is needed for general assistance.

If you enjoy caring for people, something along the lines of senior services or in-home care could be your ticket to a rich and rewarding career. The fact that you cannot devote full-time energy to the project initially may cost you some customers, but your after-hours schedule will fit the needs of many people. I believe that this is a solid foundation to build a moonlighting business on, and it is one that probably will continue to grow.

PETS AND ANIMALS

If you like pets and animals, you are sure to find some moonlighting money by caring for them when their owners are away. Pet-sitting is often much more profitable than baby-sitting. Training dogs is another way to make money with furry critters. You can open a boarding kennel or a training school, or go on location as a pet-sitter.

My family has had, and does have, many pets and animals. We currently have dogs, cats, and pheasants. We have had pigs, horses, goats, chickens, frogs, birds, and a variety of other natural elements in and around our home. For us to go away for a few days is a major problem in terms of caring for the creatures. A long vacation is almost out of the question. I am living proof of the need for pet-sitters.

If you are willing to drive to the homes of people who have pets and care for the animals after you get off work, you can make pretty good money. In many cases, you will only be feeding and providing water for the pets. Some customers may want you to take the animals for a walk. The types of animals that you tend can range from iguanas to horses. Even though you are not boarding the animals, you can charge more for your services than if you were. Let me explain.

I have a dog as a pet. If I were to leave for a period of time, I would have to either board Travis or have someone come by my home to take care of him. The boarding fees charged by veterinarians and other kennels are expensive. But I would pay more to have someone care for Travis in his normal surroundings. I don't like the idea of my dog being caged in a little wire crate. If you will come to my place and feed and water him, I'll pay more than I would to simply put him up in a pet motel. Many pet owners feel the same way. This is great for you. There is no kennel overhead for your business. You are an on-location care provider who makes more than the people who pay high rent and start-up costs for kennels. It does work this way, and you can take advantage of it.

CLEANING UP

Cleaning up after other people is a perennial opportunity for an energetic moonlighter. The best money is usually in commercial work, but residential cleaning pays fairly well, too. The money you can make will vary, depending on the types of customers you work for and where you work. As a moonlighter, commercial cleaning is good to seek out for two reasons. It normally pays more than residential work, and it is almost always performed after normal business hours. This is perfect for the moonlighter who works a regular job during the day.

You don't have to invest much money to start your own cleaning company. Many residential customers provide their own cleaning tools, equipment, and supplies. Commercial companies sometimes do, but you probably will need to invest in a strong vacuum cleaner and some basic cleaning equipment and supplies if you seek commercial work.

If you decide to set up a cleaning company, you generally will need a business license and some liability insurance, and you may need to get bonded. None of this is difficult to obtain or do, and it's usually not expensive. You can solicit customers with direct mail, personal visits, or ads in local newspapers. The overhead for operating a cleaning business is low, and the profit potential is good.

Once you have a stable of customers, you won't have to continue paying for advertising. By word of mouth, your business reputation will get around. Satisfied customers will remain customers, and you will have a steady routine for your moonlighting.

Offices and homes are not the only places where you can clean up for cash. Hotels and motels might enter into contracts with you. These types of places often maintain staffs to do cleaning and housekeeping, but there may be something else for you to do. If you can obtain a few service contracts with hotels and motels, you may not have the time, or the need, to clean anywhere else.

What comes to your mind when you think of cleaning? You probably think about vacuuming, dusting, washing dishes, or other jobs of this nature. Don't look at cleaning services with tunnel vision. There is much more opportunity in this field than you might realize. Let me give you a few examples of what I'm talking about.

A job that is not for everyone, but that can be very profitable, is cleaning chimneys. If you live in a part of the country where wood is used to heat homes, there are a lot of chimneys that should be cleaned each year. This is dirty work that can be dangerous. If you don't like the idea of walking around on the roofs of buildings, forget about putting on the big, black top hat. However, this is a job that you can do in the early evenings and on weekends. Once you develop a customer list, you should enjoy return business each year.

If you prefer to keep both feet on the ground, consider buying a power-washing machine. You can use this equipment to clean the siding on homes. It also can be used to clean boats, travel trailers, motor homes, and other recreational vehicles. A trailer-mounted power washer can be taken almost anywhere, so you can offer on-site service to people. You might receive service contracts with malls to wash their exterior walls with your equipment. Cleaning parking lots is another possibility to consider. To recap, the list of cleaning opportunities is long:

- Office buildings
- Schools
- Homes
- Hotels
- Motels
- Churches
- Stores
- Chimneys
- Power washing
- Parking lots

LAWN AND GARDEN SERVICES

Lawn and garden services are good choices for moonlighters who enjoy working outdoors. Lawn and garden work may include the following:

- Grass cutting
- Garden tilling
- Lawn feeding and watering
- Leaf raking
- Snow removal
- Landscaping

You don't have to possess a muscular build and a lot of stamina to do this type of work when you have the right equipment. With today's riding lawn mowers, self-propelled tillers, and assorted other equipment, almost anyone can handle lawn and garden work, which used to be backbreaking chores.

The start-up cost for this type of business can be very low or very high, depending on what equipment you want to buy. You can cut grass with a little push mower that costs less than $100, or you can buy a riding tractor that costs several thousand dollars. There is, of course, a lot of middle ground for you to choose from.

If you don't own a truck to haul your equipment around, you will need a utility trailer. This type of vehicle usually costs around $400. Be sure to buy some liability insurance to cover your work, and you may need a special insurance policy to cover your equipment, because it is used for professional purposes.

Cutting lawns is no longer child's play. People pay a lot of money to have their lawns cut and maintained. You can extend your basic lawn services. For example, you can dethatch lawns in the fall and overseed them with new seed. You may apply treatments to lawns to make them greener and healthier. Before taking on this type of business, check with local authorities to see if you must be licensed to work with the chemicals that are being used.

In the fall, you can rake leaves and dispose of them for your customers. If you live in an area where it snows in the winter, consider buying a snowblower and offering your services to clear driveways and walkways. Once you acquire customers, it's best to get as much work as you can from them.

If you live in an area where vegetable gardens are popular, you can offer to till the soil for customers. Self-propelled, rear-tine tillers are easy to work with. There is almost no physical effort needed beyond walking behind the machine. You also can offer to prepare the soil for customers to adjust the pH level. They'll get a better garden, and the work is easy. All you need is a walk-behind broadcast spreader and the right additives, such as lime or fertilizer.

Landscaping is another big-money occupation. If you are caring for other people's lawns and gardens, you may be able to drum up some more work by offering to create flower beds and decorative planting. This work requires a little more physical effort, but the money is good. Establish yourself as a contractor with local nurseries and you should be able to buy your plants at discounted prices. Sell them at retail prices and make money for your labor and your materials.

Grow Your Own Profits

I recently saw a sign that read that all farmers have growing businesses. You, too, can operate a growing business. If you don't like the idea of cutting grass or tilling gardens, you might consider setting up your own greenhouse. If you have space on your property for a greenhouse, you can do very well growing flowers and plants for consumers, corporations, and even florists.

A small greenhouse that is not too fancy can be built for only a few hundred dollars. I've seen complete construction kits for the framework selling for less than $200. Plastic to cover the structure is also inexpensive. If you become serious about growing, you will need fan cooling, heat, moisture control, and other such equipment—and the cost goes up considerably. But for a part-time moonlighting venture, you can get by without all the bells and whistles.

If you enjoy working with plants, you can turn your hobby into money. Raising tomatoes in a greenhouse is easy, and people will pay good prices for fresh tomatoes. It's possible to grow all types of flowers, herbs, and vegetables in a greenhouse. There is some money in this, but there is bigger money in growing plants for corporate customers.

Many businesses want plants in their offices, lobbies, and common areas. But most of these outfits don't want to bother with caring for the plants. They sometimes buy artificial plants. Many business owners rent plants and pay a monthly fee for having them cared for. This arrangement is one in which your moonlighting time and greenhouse are likely to be the most valuable.

Your first step is growing plants that can be placed in businesses. You sell or rent the plants to the business and offer it a service contract to care for the plants. This arrangement is set up a lot more often than most people realize. Your green thumb can earn you a sizable stack of greenbacks.

Even if you don't rent or sell plants, you still can offer your services as a caregiver for greenery. Watering plants, nipping off dead blossoms and leaves, and dusting leaves are just some of what you will do to earn your money. The business will want you to perform your duties when it will not be distracting to employees and customers, making this an ideal moonlighting venture. And hardly any start-up cost or overhead expense is involved in this endeavor.

WORKING WITH YOUR HANDS

If you are the type of person who enjoys working with your hands, there is almost no end to the list of services that you might offer customers. Working with your hands may involve:

- Handyman services
- Specialized trade services
- Small-engine repairs
- Appliance repairs
- Trailer services
- Security-system installations

People with specialized licenses, such as plumbers and electricians, can produce major income in a moonlighting business. Unlicensed people can do very well offering their services as handymen or fix-it persons.

Running a hands-on service business lends itself well to moonlighters. Many people work full-time jobs. It's hard for them to take time off from work to have repairs done around their homes. If you are willing to work nights and weekends at regular rates, your services become a bargain. Many full-time service companies charge overtime fees for this type of convenience. The fact that you are available at normal rates in the off-hours is a big advantage.

I've worked with my hands for decades. My most notable skill as a hands-on worker is in plumbing. I can perform many other tasks, but plumbing is the most profitable one for me. It's relatively easy for me to make more than $100 a night doing plumbing work after-hours. I don't do this a lot anymore, but I used to almost all the time. In fact, it is the way I put money together to set up a full-time business of my own many years ago.

As a business consultant, I've talked with many tradespeople who wanted to go into business for themselves. Most of them have started out as moonlighters and have grown into full-time business owners. It's not just tradespeople who do this. Some people take the same path when repairing small engines or performing body work on automobiles. Possessing the skills needed to make repairs is a good ace in the hole for hard times. Things break down, and people pay to have them fixed. It might as well be you who they are paying.

The Trades

All the trades offer opportunities for moonlighters. Carpenters, electricians, plumbers, masons, painters, and everyone else involved in the construction and repair of buildings can find evening and weekend work as independent moonlighters. Small classified ads placed in local newspapers usually produce a steady, but not abundant, flow of telephone calls. Flyers and direct mail also bring in work.

One mistake that many moonlighting tradespeople make is charging too little for their time. Don't fall into this trap. If you are a professional, charge professional rates. The fact that you are willing to work nights and weekends makes you worth every penny of regular professional rates. As an independent contractor, you are going to have some overhead expenses that must be factored into the prices you charge. Overhead is something that a lot of rookie moonlighters overlook.

I've known plumbers who made about $12 an hour at their day jobs who thought they were getting rich by charging $18 an hour for evening work. Once you factor in the cost of insurance, tools, a truck, and related business expenses, the profit is not so good as it may seem. It's silly to charge only $18 an hour for work that most plumbers are charging $40 an hour for. It's OK to charge a little less to get yourself going quickly, but don't beat yourself out of money that you deserve.

Small-Engine Repair

Small-engine repair is a popular moonlighting service. It can pay pretty well, and the work can be performed in a home garage or yard. People who are good with motors and mechanical objects can make money working on lawn mowers, snowmobiles, garden equipment, off-road vehicles, chain saws, and other small engines. There is a constant demand for this type of work, and you don't need a lot of money to get started in the business.

Once you are established, you may want to offer additional services. For example, you might sharpen blades for lawn mowers. You could buy old equipment, revitalize it, and sell the pieces as reconditioned units. If you don't mind moving around a bit, you can make house calls. If a person can call you to come work on his or her riding lawn mower at his or her home, rather than having to trailer the tractor into a shop, you're probably the person who will get the work. You can charge more for your time when you do your work on location.

Appliances

Appliances break down and people panic. If a family's washing machine dies when there are loads of clothes for the parents and children to be done, you can bet it won't be long before one of the parents is scanning the telephone book for help. If you are skilled in repairing appliances, you can build your business in two ways. Offer an in-shop price for small appliances and a more expensive labor rate for in-home service. Your biggest expense in this type of business is your inventory of parts.

Many appliance businesses charge people to haul away their old appliances. You might be able to get paid to remove people's old equipment and then recondition the pieces for resale to other customers. If you have facilities to work in, such as a garage, shed, or basement, this can be a lucrative business to get into.

A Trailer Service

A trailer service is a business that doesn't receive much publicity, but it can produce some pretty good paydays. People often need to have objects or animals trailered for one reason or another. If you own a tow vehicle and a trailer, you can make money in this field. It's not the type of moonlighting that offers steady work, but the pay is good when you work.

My daughter used to have a pony. It broke out of its corral on two occasions when it was spooked by a roaming moose. Each time, the escape occurred at night. By the time we located the pony, it was about two miles from home. The distance was too great to walk the pony home, and it was too frightened to ride. This situation left us with a problem. We didn't own a horse trailer. Without much choice in the matter, we hired a person to trailer the horse back to our house. It cost us about $75 each time, for a two-mile ride.

Not bad money for the moonlighter with the trailer and a bargain for us, considering the situation we were in.

Many people need trailers but don't own them or other vehicles set up to tow them. Some people are intimidated by the thought of towing a trailer. Even with only a simple utility trailer, you can cash in on people who need to have a big bed picked up from a store or who have to get their riding lawn mower or all-terrain vehicle into a shop for service.

Horse trailers are expensive, but utility trailers aren't. You can pick up a used utility trailer for less than $300 in my area. I've seen them advertised for half of that price. If you invest $200 in a trailer and use it only once a week, you will be making a profit very quickly.

Security Systems

It's unfortunate, but we live in a society where people are often afraid of their neighbors and of the unknown. This sparks a need for security measures. Large companies offer all types of security systems and services. You will have trouble competing with them in head-to-head competition. However, you can fill a void in the market by offering simple security-system installations during your moonlighting hours.

Your job might be as simple as installing security screws in double-hung windows. If you possess a little knowledge of wiring, you can install complete security systems for a home. Even installing deadbolt locks can compensate you well for your time. Security is a concern that continues to grow, so this should be a good, progressive market to get into. Start-up cost is minimal, and you can expand your services as you enhance your knowledge in the field.

RECREATIONAL SERVICES

Recreational services can be both fun and profitable. People are starved for outdoor fun these days, and they will pay you well to help them with their quest for entertainment. You may snicker at the thought of making money doing what most people do for fun, but you could be laughing all the way to the bank. I know of some people who make outrageous sums of money by providing recreational activities for others.

One man I know leads treasure hunters on field trips in England. A metal-detecting buddy of mine has gone on several of the outings. It's my understanding that it is not unusual for 40 customers to attend each trip. The leader leases land for the treasure hunters to scour with their metal detectors. Room and board also are provided, and transportation costs are also included in the deal. At least two expeditions of 40 people are held each year; each person pays $3,500. Forty people at $3,500 each is equal to $140,000. Multiply this by two trips a year, and you've got a gross income of $280,000.

Certainly, expenses must come out of the gross profit, quite a lot of them I assume. Even so, the money for taking people on these trips is pretty good. Using ridiculous overhead projections, it looks as if an individual could make well over $75,000 a year in salary. Keep in mind, there are only two trips a year, so much of the year is left to make other money with.

Photographers with national reputations often offer photo safaris that are similar in nature to the treasure-hunting adventures. Customers pay a package fee for transportation, lodging, food, photo opportunities, and sometimes some instruction. The amounts can be in excess of $5,000. Surely, there are a lot of details to deal with and many headaches involved, but the profit figures are off the charts.

If you get a two-week vacation from your job, you could line up a big trip during this time. Not only would you get to go away, you could be paid very well for the trip. Weekend trips are also possibilities. You can run workshops and similar events that might well pull in more money in a single weekend than you make in a month. I read about a real estate seminar where participants were charged $2,500 for a weekend, and the results turned out to be very profitable. An insurance outfit my wife knows of ran a seminar at a rate of $99 per person and pulled more than 100 people for a one-day talk. That's nearly $10,000 for a one-day event. Room cost was about $75; there were also marketing costs.

Giving a real estate seminar doesn't fit the mold of recreational activities, but it can be used as a template for success. Have you ever considered holding a weekend course in the art of fishing with a fly rod? Could you teach people to bowl in a day? What types of special knowledge do you possess that people will pay to obtain? The odds are good that you have some.

If you enjoy racquetball, you could give lessons to people who are interested in learning the sport. Maybe golf is your game and you can offer lessons at a local driving range or golf course. Do you like to ride the rapids in a raft? Put together a white-water rafting enterprise that you can run on the weekends. Something as simple as leading a nature walk can be a moneymaker. Some jurisdictions, such as the state of Maine, require a person to be licensed as a Registered Guide to lead certain expeditions. Check the local laws in your area to see if you need a license.

Of all the recreational-income opportunities available, I like the idea of leading specialized tours the most. You can take people out in canoes or go bird-watching. Customers will be happy to pay a fair price for the opportunity to go fishing on a deep-sea charter. You line up the boat and crew, and get paid for going fishing. So many outdoor possibilities are available to choose from that an entire book probably could be written about them. Decide what you enjoy most and build your business around it. If it's hiking, lead hiking and backpacking expeditions in desirable tourist locations. Maybe you will do little more than provide a shuttle service for canoes and rafts along popular rivers. A trailer with some racks on it is all you need, but it helps to have rental canoes and rafts. The point is, there is nearly no end to what you can come up with for cashing in on the outdoor craze.

Because it is possible to make such astounding money in the outdoor fields, let's discuss the principles and practices of the business. In this section, we will concentrate on guided tours, lectures, and organized events. You don't even have to be there. You could hire outdoor experts to put on the show for you. The profit that you reap could be the reward of a general contractor, for lack of a better description. In other words, you set everything up and run it from home, while on-site people take care of your customers, and you receive a bulk of the income for being the promoter.

Being a promoter is like being a real estate broker or a general contractor. You bring people together to affect a successful deal. The work you do isn't necessarily the primary source of the income, but you get a piece of the action for putting all the pieces together. The commission rate can be very attractive. In fact, let's look at a couple of scenarios that might play out for you.

Because I live in Maine, I'll give you an idea for the Northeast. Let's assume that you want to capture the interest of photographers. Your customers, as you see them, are wildlife and outdoor photographers. To attract your customers, you are going to place ads on the Internet and in specialty magazines, such as those catering to photographers and people who enjoy outdoor activities. Here's the way you should direct your offer.

Outdoor enthusiasts and photographers are invited to join you and your team on a very special outing. The first day will be spent on a boat, going out to see seals and puffins. Photo opportunities will exist, and you and your team will help with tips on how to capture the creatures on film. The next day will be spent watching and photographing whales. Lodging and food will be provided, but people are responsible for their own transportation to the lodging facility. Local transportation will be provided by shuttle vans. How does this sound so far?

Maine has many boat charters that specialize in wildlife watching, with puffins, seals, and whales ranking high on the list of attractions. Because I live in Maine, coordinating the entire package would be easy for me. I talk to the boat owners and make all the arrangements. Then I negotiate for group rates at a good lodging facility with a dining room. I arrange for bag lunches for everyone on the boat. Setting up a shuttle service is easy. I just call a company that does this type of work and request my prearranged days. It happens that I am a qualified photographer, so I could give the lessons needed for amateurs, but I could just as easily hire a local photographer to do this for me.

My effort in the program is designing and placing the ads and making the local arrangements. People call me, or my answering service, and book their time with credit cards. It's a done deal. How much money can be made? It depends on the sales pitch. Realistically, if I took about 20 people on each tour, I think I could net somewhere in the neighborhood of $5,000 to $10,000 for a single weekend.

Now, let's change the program around for our second example. This time I'm going to work with a travel agency to arrange a more exotic trip. We are going to Africa for two weeks on a photo safari. Or we could just as easily be going to Hudson Bay to photograph polar bears. The actual event is only a small portion of the program.

Using the same basic profit percentages that I used in the 2-day trip, a 14-day event might pull in anywhere from $28,000 to $56,000. I'm figuring my time at $100 a day, multiplied by 20 people. That's $2,000 a day. It's very possible that a higher rate could be justified. Some of my profit is coming from discounts that I arrange on travel, food, and lodging. Because I'm the promoter, I may get a 10-percent price break and sell the plan to my clients at retail numbers. The concept works very well, and a good number of people provide this type of service regularly, which is a good indicator that it works.

On a smaller scale, you could lead expeditions on hikes, such as through the Appalachian Trail. Offering an outdoor survival camp could pull in a good deal of business, but make sure that you or your team players are experts in the field. Fishing derbies are another great way to get people to pay you to plan their fun. The list of possibilities may be endless. If you put a creative mind to work in the right way, you can come up with some staggering income from simple ideas. Keep things as easy as you can. Simple is better, most of the time. The fewer people you have involved, the less there is to go wrong. Don't get greedy. Take baby steps as you work the bugs out of your program. Once you perfect the system, you can make a darned good living as a part-time promoter.

9
REAL ESTATE REWARDS

 elling real estate has been a moonlighting job for many people over the years. Full-time salespeople are numerous, but they generally are outnumbered by part-time real estate agents. Why do so many people turn to real estate for their spare money? Because a lot of money can be made in a short time. Some real estate moonlighting possibilities include:

- Get a license and sell as an agent or broker.
- Rehab and sell existing buildings.
- Publish real estate newsletters.
- Offer house-checking services.
- Work with change-of-use properties for big profits.
- Learn to buy low and sell high.

Selling one house can easily create a part-time income in excess of $14,000. If you sell a business property, the commission can be astronomical. Big money can be made in real estate, and you don't have to be licensed as an agent or broker to make some of it. The highest returns with the least amount of risk, however, usually come to those who are licensed real estate professionals.

Selling comes naturally to some people and never to others. If you have a gift for talking with strangers, you probably can prosper in sales. You don't have to be a slick talker to make a lot of sales. In fact, it is often the slow, honest approach that results in the best sales. What you wear and drive can influence your success in sales, but even these things are not the most critical aspects of being good at selling products and services. Your personality is what is most important.

People who don't enjoy working with other people are not good candidates for sales work. But if you can strike up a conversation and keep it going with people you don't know, you could be a natural salesperson. Even if you don't work in sales now, you should weigh the option carefully. Salespeople are often some of the highest paid people in the workforce. You get paid for what you accomplish. If you work hard and are good at what you do, the money rolls in.

I mentioned that you don't have to possess a real estate license to make money in real estate. You can be your own company by buying and selling real estate yourself. If you're thinking that you can't do this because you don't have much money, read on. It's very possible to make large sums of money in real estate without using much cash. Let me give you an example of a true case history.

As the owner of a real estate brokerage, I work with investors. My customers and clients buy apartment buildings, land, and buildings for business uses. They also buy run-down homes to fix up for a profit. A few years ago, I found a house that was being used as a duplex. On checking the zoning, I found that the house could be remodeled to accommodate up to five rental units. A building with five apartments is worth much more than a building with two apartments.

Once I realized how profitable this property could be, I called some of my investors to tell them about it. The second one I called wanted to see it. After inspecting the property and confirming what I had found out regarding the zoning, the investor offered a contract to the seller. I think the cash deposit was only $100. The contract was accepted and the investor had the right, by contract, to assign the contract to someone else if he wanted to. A date for closing was set to take place in 60 days or less.

Once the property was under contract, the investor listed it with me to sell to someone else. In less than a week, another investor bought the contract from the first investor. The first investor made about $10,000 for putting a small deposit on the property and offering it for sale. The second investor closed on the contract and converted the building. His equity position in the building shot way up. Everyone was happy. So you see, it's possible to make big money with little money when you know how to do it.

In this chapter, we are going to discuss many ways for you to make money in real estate. Some ways require a license, while others don't. We can't go into great detail, but many other books are available on the subject. I've written several of them. We will start with the traditional ways of working with real estate and wind down the chapter with more creative ways. You are sure to find something that interests you.

REAL ESTATE LICENSE LAWS

Real estate license laws vary from state to state. Some states are easy to get licensed in, while others are more difficult. Depending on where you work, you may have to complete a heavy schedule of continuing education to maintain your license. Not all states have this requirement. In general, you must check the local license laws to find out exactly what pertains to you. However, I can give you a general description of what you might expect.

I'm licensed as a designated broker, which is the highest classification available in Maine. Someone just entering the field of real estate, in Maine, would be a salesperson. The next step up would be an associate broker. The next level is a broker. Finally, you reach the status of designated broker, when you own or manage a brokerage.

To become a licensed salesperson, you probably will have to take a written test. Many companies offer training courses to prepare you for the test. Once licensed as a salesperson, you are required to work under the supervision of a broker or designated broker, depending on where you live and work. Some states require certain amounts of time at each classification before you can step up. These steps allow you to gain experience as you move up the ladder.

When you work for a brokerage, typically you split your commission with the brokerage. There is no set rule about the split, but a 50–50 split is common. If you made a sale that produced a $10,000 commission to your brokerage, you might get $5,000 and the brokerage might get $5,000. Some brokerages work on different principles. For example, you might pay office rent and related business expenses out of your own pocket to the brokerage and retain a much larger share of your commission. Once you are licensed to operate your own brokerage, all the commission stays in your pocket.

How Much Money?

How much money can you make selling real estate? You are limited only by your personal success. Some full-time brokers make less than $20,000 a year, while others make more than $200,000. It has been said that 20 percent of the salespeople make 80 percent of the money. I don't doubt this one bit. Of course, your earnings will be relative to the prices of real estate in your area.

A commission usually is based on a percentage of a sales price. If, for instance, you were to earn a 7-percent commission on a sale, you would make a lot more money selling $200,000 homes than you would selling $60,000 homes if you sold the same number of homes. Real estate commissions in my area average between 6 percent and 7 percent of the sales price. So, selling a $100,000 home could result in maybe a $7,000 commission.

When you project your potential earnings, remember to allow for splits with your brokerage and cobrokerages. This can burst your bubble, but it has to be acknowledged. Let me give you an example of what I mean. Assume that you are working with a brokerage on a 50–50 split. You find a buyer who is willing to purchase a house that is listed with a different brokerage. The total commission is $6,000. When the sale is closed, the listing brokerage probably will get $3,000. Your brokerage also should receive $3,000. But you're going to wind up with only $1,500. Until you have your own brokerage, you must be willing to split up your money with other people.

You can receive benefits for what you pay in splits. The brokerage should be paying all your basic business expenses, such as your office and telephone use. Advertising also should be paid for by the brokerage. Many other operating expenses are absorbed by the brokerage, so your splits are not all profit for the brokerage.

Even if your commission on a house is only $1,500, it can add up by the end of the year. Sell one house a month and you make $18,000. Not bad for moonlighting on a small scale. Can you actually sell one house a month? It depends on you, your brokerage, and the market, but it's certainly very possible.

If you list and sell a property, your commission usually doubles. By listing a house, I'm talking about when you get a home seller to agree to let your brokerage be the selling broker. Selling your own listings means that no other brokerage is involved, so the commission doesn't have to be split so many times. And if someone else sells a home that you listed, you still get a commission. If you know a lot of people or are not afraid to call strangers, you could spend all your time listing and let other people do all the selling.

Many professional brokers decide to be known as listers or sellers. Some do both, but most have a preference. My preference is being a seller. A lot of brokers prefer to be listers. You can make your own decision after you have tried a little of both, and maybe you will continue to do both. There is certainly more money, on a per-sale basis, to be made when you sell your own listings.

GETTING STARTED

Getting started as a licensed real estate professional can be confusing. It's not really difficult, but you may need some guidance. Before you take the licensing test, I strongly suggest that you attend a class or course that will prepare you for the examination. The test can be both difficult and tricky. A lot of people fail on their first few attempts. Don't underestimate what you are getting into. Take a test-preparation course. It doesn't cost much, and it's well worth your time.

Some brokerages offer preparation courses in return for your commitment to work with them once you are licensed. This isn't a bad deal, but read the fine print to see just how much the "free" course may cost you down the road. It probably will be a clean deal, but check to make sure you are not making a commitment that will hurt you later.

Once you are licensed, shop for a brokerage to work for. Don't just answer the first help-wanted advertisement you see and hang your license at that brokerage. Choosing a brokerage to work with is a lot like choosing a spouse to spend your life with. Getting hooked up with a bad brokerage can be devastating to your career.

I strongly recommend that you interview with several brokerages before you make a commitment.

When you do hang up your license with a brokerage, you should be all set to earn some serious money. A sales manager or designated broker should guide you along the path to success. Don't expect the trip to be a fast one. It can take months to get your first sale, and then a month or two more to get paid for it. Going into real estate sales is a move that you must be willing to invest time in and be patient with. Once you get sales rolling over, though, the money can be fantastic.

TRICKS OF THE TRADE

You will want to learn certain tricks of the trade to make the most money possible as a licensed real estate professional. Hopefully, your managers will share insights with you, but they may not. I'll give you a few hints to get you started on the right track.

New salespeople's activity is mostly pulling desk duty. This is when you sit in the brokerage office and answer the telephone and greet walk-in traffic. You will obtain some sales opportunities doing this. As a moonlighter, you have a better shot at some sales than daytimers do. Many people looking for homes don't become active until after normal working hours and on weekends. If this is when you are running the desk, you can receive some good leads. Desk duty, however, is rarely where the most money is made. It's a good place to start but not a good place to stay.

To make money in real estate sales, you must be aggressive by actively soliciting buyers and sellers to work with. You can do this with print advertising, direct mail, and cold calling. Pull your desk duty, but spend other time soliciting customers. If you get your hair cut or styled, talk to the people there. Hand out business cards. Leave flyers if the business will allow you to do so. Everyone you talk to is a potential customer or client. Let them know that you are a real estate professional and tell them about your services.

Enclose business cards with your checks when you pay bills. You never know when the recipient may be thinking about buying or selling a house. Get your name in front of as many people as possible. If you sit around and wait for the telephone to ring, you may find that you can't even pay the telephone bill. Get active. Be aggressive but not obnoxious.

Once you get a feel for the business, consider choosing a specialty. You might specialize in selling apartment buildings. First-time buyers may be your market. New construction is another specialty area. Find out in what area you are the most comfortable, and the most knowledgeable, and go for it.

Read books on real estate. Listen to cassette tapes offered by successful salespeople. Attend seminars. The more you do to set yourself apart from the crowd, the better your chances will be of becoming one of the 20 percent who sell 80 percent of the property. It's a good business to work in, and you can earn more money than you might ever imagine possible. But you have to work for what you get, so stay busy. Far too many salespeople are lazy. You can leave this group in the dust if you are willing to make things happen instead of waiting for them to happen.

WITHOUT A LICENSE

What can you do in real estate without a license? Many people may tell you that there isn't much that you can do, but I disagree. Some risk is involved, but the financial rewards offset it. If you are willing to roll up your sleeves and take an active interest in your work, you can make a lot of money doing conversion and repair work on properties that you buy cheap. Even if you don't have the money or the credit line to buy properties yourself, you can cash in on this lucrative aspect of real estate.

In my first big real estate deal, I bought a run-down house to call home. It was a two-story house in a borderline neighborhood. Many of the houses in the area were being renovated and sold to new owners who would, in time, improve the social standing of the community. My wife and I were living in an apartment and wanted a home of our own. We didn't have much money, but I was handy with tools and familiar with various construction trades. The house was priced right, so we bought it. We intended to fix it up and sell it for a profit.

During the renovation work on our house, we lived with dust and disarray, but we were building significant equity as we did the work ourselves. Instead of paying rent, we were buying a house. These weren't the best conditions in the world to live under, but they were more than tolerable. During this project, I got an idea and set to work on it.

If I could buy, renovate, and sell one house for a profit, it seemed that I could do the same with more houses and make more money. There was a problem, however. I didn't have enough money or credit to buy or rehab another house until I finished the one we were living in. Being impatient, I decided to find an investor who would become my partner.

It took me only a few days to find a CPA who was willing to work deals with me. I was to find suitable houses for renovation. Once I found the houses and received estimates from subcontractors on the costs to renovate the place, I would take the deals to the CPA. Local real estate appraisers would tell us what the present and future value of the homes would be. If the numbers were encouraging, the CPA would buy the properties and finance the construction work. My job, then, would be to act as a general contractor and to do as much of the work myself as was practical. When the houses were sold, the profits would be split evenly.

It took me less than two weeks to put the first deal together. We bought a small house in the same neighborhood where my house was. In about six weeks, the renovation work was completed. Selling the house took longer than we had expected, but a sale was made, and so was a profit. My partner and I continued this type of real estate work with success. Later, we started building new homes to complement our work with older houses.

Through my examples, you have seen just two ways that you can make money in real estate without a license. You can buy rundown houses yourself and fix them up for a profit, or you can put together a partnership with someone else who has more financial clout than you do. Either way, you can make tens of thousands of dollars in a relatively short period of time.

You don't have to be good with your hands to make money rehabbing old buildings. If you have good organizational skills, you can subcontract the work to others and manage the project. You will make less money as a general contractor than you would if you did the work yourself, but the profit still can be pretty good.

Buying real estate as an investment often pays off. However, failure for investors is not uncommon. Not everyone is cut out to be a wheeling, dealing, real estate investor. If you are concerned about investing your money in the purchase of real estate, there are still some ways for you to make money in real estate without possessing a sales license.

A REAL ESTATE NEWSLETTER

A different approach for making money with real estate is to produce your own real estate newsletter. You've probably seen many of these publications in local stores and supermarkets. There are two basic approaches to take with this type of publication. You can do what most publishers do and make the entire newsletter a compilation of property for sale. Or you can add informative features on real estate–related topics to make the newsletter more than just a collection of advertisements. I favor the latter, but the choice is yours.

Starting your own newsletter is not a difficult task, assuming that you have a home computer to work with. Your primary job will be soliciting advertisers. If you are good at calling people and selling your services, you can produce a profitable newsletter very quickly.

The publication should be offered to the public free of charge; your costs for preparing, printing, and distributing the newsletter must be paid for in some other way, usually with advertising. Start by contacting real estate companies in your area. Offer them a free advertisement for one issue to prove that your publication will work for them. Running free ads means that you are going to have to absorb the cost of production and distribution for your first issue out of your own pocket. But the maneuver is worth it. Once you get a few major real estate companies to agree to advertise with you, even though they are not paying for the ad space, you can tell other potential customers that so-and-so will be advertising in your premiere issue. You don't have to give away all the ads in your first issue, but give away enough of them to attract some well-known companies. You build credibility and get other businesses to follow the lead of their competitors.

Once you get the ball rolling, selling advertising to additional companies is not very difficult, especially after you have published an issue or two that you can show prospective advertisers. When they see samples of your newsletter, they will be more inclined to sign an advertising contract.

Real estate companies are your logical targets for advertising, but don't think that they are your only sources of revenue. Many companies cater to real estate transactions, and they might like some exposure in your newsletter. Banks that provide financing to home buyers are good prospects. Title insurance companies, real estate attorneys, appraisers, individual real estate brokers and agents, and insurance companies that sell homeowner's insurance are all good candidates for your advertising sales. A number of other types of businesses, of course, such as plumbing companies, home-inspection companies, and so forth may pay to have an ad appear in your publication.

Once you have made all the commercial contacts you can, start working on people who are trying to sell their homes without a broker. Look for for-sale-by-owner ads in your local newspapers. Call the people and make them aware of your specialized newsletter. You will face some rejection, but you will also acquire several new advertisers.

The potential for advertisers is vast. Making money in this way with real estate is one of the safest ways that I know of to capitalize on real estate without much risk. You can sell your advertising during off-hours, and putting a newsletter together on a computer is easy. Getting your issues printed is simple, and distribution can be handled after-hours. Here is a very plausible moonlighting opportunity that could make more money for you than you make at your present, full-time job.

If you want to produce a newsletter that is more than just a collection of ads, you will need text pertaining to real estate. You could research articles and write them yourself, but there is an easier way to obtain them, and you can probably get paid for publishing them! Most of your advertisers will be linked to the real estate industry in one way or another, meaning that your advertisers are good sources of useful information on the subject of real estate. Offer them a deal that they can't refuse.

Let's say that one of your advertisers is a lawyer. How would the lawyer feel if you offered him or her an entire column in the newsletter? Mr. or Ms. Lawyer's column would be a form of distinction and credibility. You charge the lawyer for running the column, but at the same time, the lawyer gets a byline as your publication's expert on real estate law. It's great publicity for the attorney.

You usually will have bankers advertising with you. Offer one of them the same type of "advertorial" column. Insist in all cases that the material used is beneficial to readers on a wide range and not just a tooting of one's own horn. You will be receiving good copy for your newsletter and will be getting paid to print it. This line of attack could continue with each type of professional involved in real estate transactions. Before you know it, your newsletter will contain columns from experts in all fields, and you will be getting paid to publish them. This is great!

House-Checking Services

A house-checking service is another way to make money in real estate. House checking involves routinely checking vacant homes for heat, damage, cosmetic needs, and other maintenance problems. If you live in an area where people take long vacations, such as Maine, you can do pretty well with this type of business. Many people in Maine head south for the winter. Their homes are vacant. You could make daily or weekly inspections of the properties to make sure that they remain in good shape.

A lot of people go on vacation for a week or two at a time. Your house-checking service could cater to them. Your job could be to bring in the mail and newspapers. Maybe you could move cars around in the driveway and turn lights on in different rooms from time to time to make the homes look occupied. Security is an important issue in these modern times, and you can cash in on it with a house-checking service.

There is one drawback to this type of service. You might come upon a burglar during your checks, so the work could get dangerous. While this is unlikely, it is worth considering. On the whole, though, house checking is a great opportunity for moonlighters, and the pay can be pretty good. Combine pet-sitting with your house-checking, and the profit grows even larger.

If you don't like the idea of selling real estate or working with property, you might enjoy selling other services that you may be able to offer. Almost everyone has some traits that people will pay to have access to. The next chapter covers some of these areas.

10
SELLING YOURSELF

Many business owners sell products, but maybe you should think of selling yourself. This chapter outlines ways to sell your personal knowledge in some form, such as teaching or consulting. Some people make very high incomes working as consultants. You probably can earn steady money teaching a certain class several nights a week. Many possible options are available for you to consider when it comes to cashing in on your personal experiences and knowledge.

I'm no college professor, but I have served as adjunct faculty for Central Maine Technical College. Teaching two classes a week, one night for each class, provided me with enough extra cash to pay for a good portion of my housing expense. With the money I could make two car payments each month. All I had to do was teach a total of five hours a week. The work was easy and fun.

What were my credentials for teaching classes? I'm a licensed master plumber. One of the classes I taught was a code class that prepared prospective plumbers for their licensing exams. The other class was a plumbing apprentice class, in which I taught students the basics of plumbing. I might just as well have been teaching a photography class or a class on real estate or construction. I suppose I could have booked myself to teach five nights a week if I'd chosen to do so. The hourly rate I was paid didn't measure up to what I could make in my own businesses, but it was a lot more than what most employers in my area pay their workers. I taught to help the community, to gain some new experience as a teacher, and to see if I would enjoy going on a seminar trail. You could do this for any number of reasons, but extra money is never a bad reason.

I know I've mentioned previously that I work with owners of small businesses as a consultant. This is not my primary source of income, so you could say it is a form of moonlighting for me. After having been in business for myself most of my life, there is much that I have to offer people who are either in business for themselves or who want to go into business for themselves. I don't hold a degree in business from a college or any other degrees. What I bring to the table is hard-earned, real-world experience.

Customers place their sense of value on what you have to offer based on what you can truly do for them. Only a few people will be concerned about your college pedigree. The proof is in the pudding, and if you've got the track record to prove your expertise, you don't need the documents on the wall. I have nothing against college graduates, and I often have regretted not going to college myself. Certainly, I want both of my children to be educated in higher learning. My lack of formal education, however, has rarely gotten in the way of my success, and my self-taught skills are as effective as any I've seen. The point is this: if you don't have a degree, don't count yourself out as a consultant or teacher. It's what you know and can share that is important, not how you came to know it.

BECOMING A CONSULTANT

Becoming a consultant usually is as simple as obtaining a business license and offering your services to the public. Few, if any, jurisdictions have complex licensing requirements for consultants. I know a man who worked in California on computer development who offers consulting services in Maine. A man in Washington State offers consulting on communication issues. My consulting revolves around small business start-up and success. If you look deeply into the folds of consulting, I'm sure you can find consultants for just about every imaginable subject. Where do you fit into the picture?

To decide if you have a future as a consultant, you must look at what you have to offer the public. If you know a lot about financing, you might become a consultant to home buyers, business owners, or anyone else who wishes to obtain a loan. When your past experience has taught you to do magical things with computers, you can hire yourself out as a computer consultant. Credit collection is a big problem for many business owners. If you have a background as a credit manager or collection agent, you might do well soliciting work in collecting stale accounts. Whatever it is that you have to offer, there probably are people who are willing to pay you to share it.

Consulting work is considered white-collar employment, but you don't have to wear a suit and tie to sell yourself as a consultant. Many blue-collar job titles qualify people as professional consultants. Let's consider an instance in which a blue-collar worker, a carpenter, wants to become a consultant. How can this be accomplished? First of all, the carpenter may possess additional skills that lend themselves to a consulting field. In the rare event that the only knowledge this carpenter has to sell is carpentry, there is still room for consulting. In this example, our carpenter's name is Bruce. He has years of experience in both commercial and residential work. After breaking his leg in a bad fall from a roof, Bruce was looking for a way to make some money while his leg heals. He decided to become a consultant. What can he do and who will his clients be?

Because we are assuming that Bruce has only his carpentry skills to sell, he is limited in his scope. In real life, this is rarely the case. Most people have many areas of expertise from which to draw. Bruce has read about becoming a consultant, but he's not sure where to start. Then he read an idea book that gave him direction. It's the kind of book you are reading now.

All of a sudden, Bruce had a wealth of ideas in front of him. He could meet with home owners to discuss their remodeling plans. People will pay for professional, outside advice on big-ticket expenses, such as major remodeling. Because Bruce was not bidding a job, he had no reason to be biased in what he advised his clients. Bruce could be a project manager for the construction of new homes. His position as a project manager/consultant could save customers thousands of dollars compared to what they would have to pay a general contractor. The home owners were their own general contractors, relying on Bruce's advice as needed.

Bruce found that it was difficult to break into commercial jobs, because so many of these jobs are supervised by architects. However, he found an opening on the commercial scene to act as a labor consultant to the carpentry contractors. Bruce's experience in running large work crews came in handy for these contractors, and they paid him for advice and possibly for some on-site supervision.

Another idea that Bruce came up with was offering quality-control inspections for jobs in progress. Bruce is not a working contractor, so he can inspect the work of others without any reason to mislead customers. But Bruce's big break came when he received a call from a theatrical company that wanted Bruce to consult with them on the construction of stage sets. This was where Bruce found the biggest money, and now he specializes in planning and supervising stage sets all over the country. He never went back to hammering nails.

You could say Bruce was a lucky guy, but luck plays little part in it. By researching what he had to sell and where it might be sold, Bruce created a new life for himself. A man who used to swing a hammer in sweltering heat moved up the ladder of success several notches. But how does this work out for white-collar workers?

In our next example, we have a professional person who has been employed as a systems analyst for a major nonprofit corporation. She is a whiz at computers and loves working with them. Marcy was in a serious car accident that left her disabled for handling the responsibilities of her job. She experienced months of depression. Finally, she decided to fight back as an independent computer consultant. From that day on, she had more fun, made more money, and lived a better life than ever before. Here's how it all worked out.

After Marcy's accident, she was unable to work with a computer screen for long intervals. The focus and concentration that was required gave her severe headaches. She still possessed her superb skills, but she was unable to use them as a full-time employee in the position that she held at the time of the accident. When Marcy decided to become an independent consultant, her parents were supportive, but skeptical.

Marcy's previous employer, who had filled her position because Marcy was unable to return to work full-time, retained her as an outside consultant. Other nonprofit organizations in the community also contracted Marcy to help them with their computer needs. The new consulting business was growing, but Marcy wanted more. She contacted local computer stores and made them aware of her services. In just a few months, Marcy was working a full schedule as a consultant and making nearly twice what she had made at her old job.

The examples you've just read are fictitious, but they are based on true case histories of people I've known. In both cases, the people were injured and forced to find another way to make themselves worthwhile in a financial sense. Sometimes it takes a tragic accident to spur people out of their comfort zone. You, however, don't have to wait to be hurt to capitalize on your potential as a consultant. I've shown you, briefly, how both blue-collar and white-collar workers can do it in a generic sense. Now let me show you how you can apply basic principles to do it yourself.

EVALUATING YOUR SALABLE QUALITIES

One of the first steps to becoming a successful consultant is evaluating your salable qualities. This should be an easy thing to do, but many people have trouble with it. Far too many people sell themselves short. Don't fall into this trap. To start with, you will need paper and a pen or pencil.

Sit down and decide what you enjoy doing. Write the answers down on paper. Consider your past professional history. What types of work have you performed long enough to become accomplished in the field? Once you complete your work history, look at your hobby interests. I've been a photographer since I was a child. While I'm not a household name when it comes to photography, my many years of professional experience as a moonlighter have provided me with a depth of knowledge that is valuable. Maybe you have done the same thing with some other type of hobby. For example, if you are an avid golfer, you might attempt a moonlighting career as a trainer at local courses and driving ranges.

When you are making your list, don't ignore anything. Even little aspects of your experience can be building blocks toward your work as a consultant. Not all consultants are generalists, and they shouldn't be. I consult with people on small-business matters. My work is well rounded but far from conclusive of all issues. I'm not a defined expert on labor relations and laws. The basics are a part of my program, but I'm not qualified to provide extensive advice in this area. Securing government contracts is something that I've done, but I'm no expert in the field. I know of a man, a fellow author, who is an expert in this field. He offers his consulting services on the subject. While I can't compete with him when it comes to government contracts, there are other aspects of business where he can't compete with me. For example, I know the construction trades very well, which makes me an ideal business consultant for contractors. The point is this: you more than likely have both general and specialized knowledge to pull from. Find out what it is.

Once you have a complete list of what you feel may be qualities that other people will pay you to share, you must weed through the crop. Maybe your hobby as a gardener makes you an excellent candidate as a consultant to gardeners in your area. Your infatuation with engines and auto racing could serve you well in the consulting field. Questions for your list might include:

- What activities do you enjoy?
- What have you accomplished professionally?
- What are your hobby interests?
- What areas do you feel qualified in?
- What is your strongest ability?
- Do you want to sell your knowledge?

Look over your list and pick three choices that you feel are your strongest assets. Key in on those qualities. Don't trash the other ideas, but do put them on a back burner.

Market Surveys

Once you have solid ideas for your consulting business, you must conduct a market survey to see how viable your ideas are. Big corporations will spend major money on this type of research. You don't have to. A week of telephone calls can give you a pretty good reading on what's hot and what's not. You also can get some idea of the market from reviewing the advertisements in your local telephone directory and newspapers. If there are dozens of advertisements within your area of expertise, the competition is probably too fierce for a moonlighter. On the other hand, if there is no competition, there may be no demand. Somewhere between the two extremes is ideal.

Testing

Testing the market is easy. Let's say that you are the avid golfer I spoke of previously. You've decided that you want to become a golf consultant. You're not a retired professional and you've never won a professional tournament. However, your skills can still attract clients. There are a great number of fields on which you are judged on your present ability, not on your past accomplishments.

To test the waters, you could call local golf courses, country clubs, and driving ranges to see if they would be interested in offering golf lessons to their customers. If they show any interest, you can arrange a personal interview to show them how good you are, both at golf and at giving helpful advice. Great golfers are not all good teachers. If you possess both skills, you are way out in front in the race for being the local trainer.

When you contact the various facilities, you should point out how they will make more money and make their customers happier at the same time. In fact, they probably will attract new customers by having you teach a few nights a week or on weekends.

This is an ideal situation for a moonlighter. Some consulting work will require you to work during normal business hours, but many variations lend themselves better to after-hours work.

You may land a job where you work exclusively for one club. Or you might work two nights a week at one place, one night a week at another, and weekends at yet another. You will be doing what you love to do, and getting paid well for it. Of course, your employer will take a piece of the pie for providing the facility and customers, but you will still do OK.

If you strike out with the clubs and courses, you can go straight to the consumers. Put up flyers in golf shops and stores that sell golfing equipment. Post notices in chain stores and other public places. Let the public know that you are offering golf lessons in the evenings and on weekends. You can get around your lack of references and high-grade credentials by offering a money-back guarantee if the customer isn't satisfied. Placing ads in the local newspapers, probably in the sports section, is another way to drum up business. You could even rent a mailing list of known owners of golf clubs (the type you hit balls with) and make your pitch by direct mail.

You might not think of teaching people to correct their golf swing as a form of consulting, but it is. It's important that you open your mind and let all your creative juices flow. There are so many ways to make money as a moonlighter that you can't fail. It's just a matter of finding what is best for your circumstances. Some of these personal opportunities include:

- Become a consultant.
- Teach painting classes.
- Teach aerobics.
- Train dogs.
- Lead bird-watching expeditions.
- Teach photography workshops.

- Teach writing workshops.
- Give horseback-riding lessons.

The Business Market

If you want to work in the business market as a consultant, you will have easier access to your potential customers, but your work schedule may get in the way. For example, if your job is training employees on how to use new computer software, you may have trouble doing this outside of normal business hours. Possibly, you could conduct the actual training in the evenings or on a Saturday, but you are going to have to pitch your services and win the contract during normal hours most of the time. You might be able to solicit the work with direct mail and return calls on your lunch break or right after work to clear this hurdle. But business owners and managers probably won't set meetings with you after the close of business to make a deal.

Most consultants go for the business market, because it is more lucrative and more easily targeted than general consumers. You may not attract big businesses as clients, but you may not be affected if you concentrate on small businesses, as I do.

Many of my consulting clients have fewer than 30 employees. A lot of them have no more than one employee. The business owners are busy making money during the day, so they are more accessible in the early evening, and they are prime targets for moonlighters. You can approach this market successfully when trying to hit big corporations frequently will result in failure.

Assuming that you are working on your local level, with personal presentations, you probably will be most successful if you concentrate on businesses with less than 10 employees. Of course, no cookie-cutter formula can be applied. You have to test the market and see for yourself what you are up against. Another alternative is to become a long-distance consultant, and this can work very well for moonlighters.

Long-Distance Moonlighters

Long-distance moonlighters can cheat the clock. I live and work on the East Coast. Some of my work involves companies on the West Coast. There is a three-hour time difference between the two workplaces. If I were doing my work with West Coast people as a moonlighter, I would have it made. My after-hours work would coincide with their normal business hours. When I would get off at 5:00 P.M., it would be only 2:00 P.M. on the other coast. This opens a good door to long-distance moonlighting. If you are dealing with other countries, such as Japan, the same type of time difference allows you flexibility as a moonlighter.

Conducting business by long distance is easier now than you might think. With e-mail, modems, fax machines, and next-day delivery services, you can cater to clients from far away with speed that was once possible only on the local level. This new technology, of course, broadens your potential customer base. You win two ways, with more flexible hours and with more people to do business with.

What types of consulting can you do from a distance? It depends on your skills. I work as a writer and as a technical editor without ever going into the offices of my publishers. Many of the editors who edit my books are freelancers, and they may never set foot in a publisher's office. You could be an advertising consultant without having to meet personally with your clients. Proofs and tear sheets could go back and forth by mail, fax, or computer.

Consulting is usually thought of as a one-on-one type of business, where face-to-face meetings are normal, but it doesn't have to be this way. Granted, you probably can't improve a person's golf swing very well from 500 miles away, but you could troubleshoot a computer from that distance. Don't let the fact that you live in a rural area poison you on the idea of accessing big business as a consultant. Modify your approach to compensate for your situation, and you can do very well.

CONSUMER CONSULTING

Consumer consulting is not generally so profitable as working with businesses, but it can be easier work to get. There are also a lot more people in the world than there are businesses, so your odds of scoring, in terms of percentages, are better when you work the consumer market. What you lose in inflated hourly rates might be regained in volume. However, you may have to modify your description of what consulting is. Things you should do before you jump into consulting include:

- Conduct a market survey.
- Test the market.
- Assess both the business and consumer markets.
- Decide if you want to work in a niche market.
- Consider long-distance consulting.
- Evaluate possibilities on the Internet.

In some consumer markets, consulting is a good word to use for what you do. For example, if you are an expert in credit repair, financing, and similar fields, you could bill yourself out as a credit consultant. But would you advertise your services to help people with their backhands in tennis as a tennis consultant? Not likely. You could be an interior consultant, but an interior designer is a more accepted term. You could offer your services as a math consultant to students, but the term tutor probably would work better. Tie your title to what you do in a way that the public can associate with quickly and easily.

Training and *development* are two words that have been popular for the past few years. These are just other names for consulting. So is teaching, tutoring, coaching, and so forth. In a broad sense, it is all a matter of consulting. When you share your knowledge or ability with others, you are working as a consultant. In writing this book, I'm being a consultant to all of my readers. Loosen up your definitions and you will see how wide the consulting market really is.

Consumers cannot, or will not, usually pay the high hourly fees for consulting that major corporations will. If you go to someone's home and set up a computer system, it's unlikely that you are going to get the same amount of money that you would receive for setting up a system in a large insurance business. Thus, you have to make up for the difference in volume.

Finding 100 companies to set up on a computer system on a single Saturday would be tough to do. Getting 100 consumers to come to your seminar on how to lose weight, how to quit smoking, how to succeed in real estate, or how to open their own business isn't so difficult. The net result may be the same amount of money earned between commercial and consumer work, but volume is your friend on the consumer end.

NICHE MARKETS

Niche markets are usually the best ones to concentrate on when you are dealing with consumers. Personally, I feel that they are the best ones to concentrate on across the board. If your skills are the type that will enhance certain aspects of the lives people live, you could get rich, and quick. Don't count on it, but you could. Even if you don't hit the jackpot, you can make some serious moonlighting money.

There are two sides of the coin to look at when you consider teaching, training, and consulting. Offering your services to adult education facilities as an instructor is one way to cash in on the consumer market. The money is not so good as it could be if you run your own show, but you have no marketing cost and no risk, and it may be worth taking a little less money. As we move through various niche markets, remember that most of them can be handled on your own or in conjunction with some facility that will pay you as an instructor, assuming that you are qualified to teach the subject matter.

Painting Classes

If you enjoy painting and are good at it, you could train others in the art of painting. This endeavor can grow into a pretty large business. I know a man in Maine who is a sign painter and a financial adviser. In addition to wearing those two hats, he also offers painting classes in the evenings and on weekends. The man sells art supplies to complement his studio business. You could take this type of concept and run with it. You might even make arrangements with owners of art supply stores to be their in-house trainer. The stores could offer courses that would bring in new customers, and you could be paid an hourly fee for your teaching. This mode of operation eliminates the risk for you and increases business for the owner of the store. There are so many ways to create win-win situations in this field that it's hard to fail.

Aerobics

How would you like to get paid to exercise? You can as an aerobics instructor. Whether you promote your own classes or teach students at local health spas, you can make money leading aerobics classes. Teaching aerobics is a good job for evenings and weekends, when more people are available to burn off those calories.

Dogs

We talked about training and development, but have you considered training dogs? Many dog owners pay to have their canines trained for obedience. Hunting is another area dogs often are trained for. If you like working with dogs and have a little green space to work with, you can start your own training facility. I know a man in my area who charges, on average, about $500 to train a dog. From my conversations with the man, the work doesn't take long when a trainer knows what needs to be accomplished. I don't have any firsthand experience in this field professionally, but it looks like one that dog lovers should consider. The start-up cost is minimal, but some space is needed to work the dogs, and you may need some type of license, depending on where you are working.

Bird-Watching

Bird-watching is an activity that a large number of people enjoy. If you are something of a naturalist, you could profit from teaching people where to find birds and how to identify them. You could even lead expeditions for birding. This work may not sound like much of a business, but the revenue can be quite good. When I tell you that almost any interest or skill you have can be valuable, I mean it.

Photography

Photography is a passion of mine and a favorite hobby of many. If you are into photography, you can build workshops, seminars, and training sessions around your love of cameras and film. You might teach darkroom techniques or lead photo safaris in the local park. It's not necessary to be a practicing professional to pull customers for your training sessions. Show examples of your work, and if your work is good, people will pay to learn your techniques. Give darkroom classes at night and lead your outings on weekends.

Writing

Writing is something that a vast number of people enjoy and wish to pursue. The number of people who would like to see their words published is staggering. If you have skills in any aspect of the writing business, you can give classes on the subject. Poetry doesn't usually sell well for big bucks, but people will pay to learn how to write it. Nonfiction is easier to sell than fiction, but a majority of students are more interested in writing novels. Anything that you can offer prospective writers can be worth a nice paycheck.

Riding Lessons

If you own a horse and have riding facilities, you can turn your investment into a moneymaking proposition. Give riding lessons, something that both children and adults enjoy. Trail rides and riding lessons are both very popular, and the hourly rates paid are handsome. There is some liability here, so make sure that you have adequate insurance coverage.

The List Goes On and On

The list of possibilities for selling what you know goes on and on. An entire world of people is waiting for you to let them know how you can improve their lives. Let them know what you have to offer, and you may be flooded with moonlighting work. If you need some more ideas, check out the listings in Chapter 14. If you are more inclined to sit back and receive money in your mailbox, turn to the next chapter to explore the mail-order maze.

11
THE MAIL-ORDER MAZE

The mail-order maze pulls in opportunity seekers like lights at night attract moths in summer. Millions of dollars can be made in mail order, but only a handful of entrepreneurs can navigate the maze successfully. Mail-order madness strikes people like gold fever did in the old days. If the truth were told, there are probably bigger riches to be made with mail order than there ever were for a prospector in the goldfields.

What makes people turn to mail order to make money? It's supposed to be easy. Getting rich by placing a few ads in national magazines is appealing. I must confess, I've been bitten by the mail-order bug, and so have many of my friends. While I've never hit the mother lode in mail order, I have made some money with it. Friends of mine have, too. None of us could retire on the money in our mailboxes, but it does pay for pizza and drinks. In some cases, it pays for a lot more. And it's possible that a good mail-order campaign could be more valuable than winning a lottery.

Many books have been published on the subject of making money with mail order. I've read most of them. Much of the contents are intriguing, but not conclusive. If you think about it, why would someone who is making millions of dollars in mail order reveal all the secrets to wealth? Money is made by selling books, but not the kind of money that the mail-order books indicate that you can make. Unless, of course, your mail-order enterprise is selling books.

Over the years, there have been some legendary mail-order successes. For each person who succeeded, however, thousands, if not millions, either lost money or made very little. It is true that you could be the next mail-order millionaire, but how will you achieve this status? I can't tell you how to make a million dollars with mail order, but I can share with you my experiences in the business. Some of my ideas and approaches have worked, and others have failed. All in all, I've never lost money in the game, and that's more than a lot of people can say.

The world of mail order has changed a lot since I got started in it. When I began searching for money in the mail, there was no Internet. With today's advancements in communications, both with fax machines and the Internet, the entire concept of mail-order madness has changed. The old proven ways still work, but there are new frontiers to conquer. Regardless of your media, the principles of selling by mail remain the same, and those are what we are about to explore.

SIMPLICITY

Simplicity often works best in the mail-order business. This comes as no surprise, for simplicity generally works best in most business endeavors. If you are not familiar with the cost of advertising in national magazines, you may be shocked when you see a rate card. Advertising cost usually is tied to the circulation rate of the publication you are advertising in. The prices are typically figured on a per-word price. Be prepared for some high costs if you want to advertise in major magazines.

Because the per-word cost of advertising can be very expensive, you should get your message across in as few words as possible. Paying three or four dollars per word can add up to an expensive ad if you get wordy. While you want to keep your cost down, however, it is important to provide enough information to entice people to act on your advertisement. Finding a perfect balance point is not always easy.

When you are thinking about placing ads in magazines and newspapers, you must consider the cost. You are going to have to spend money in the hopes of making money. Cutting your ads too short and receiving poor response results in financial failure. Likewise, putting in long ads that cost a small fortune is probably a waste of money. What you have to do is say enough without saying too much. It sounds simple enough, but it isn't. In the context that we are discussing, the ads in question are classified ads. We will talk about display advertising later in this chapter.

There is an easy way to bring yourself up to speed on ads that pay for themselves. You can learn from what others are doing. To do this, you must spend some time researching back issues of magazines that you wish to advertise in. A day or two at your local library can save you thousands of dollars in wasted advertising expenses.

READING THE ADS

Reading the ads in old magazines and comparing them with the ads in recent editions of the same magazines is an excellent way to see what is and what is not working for other mail-order entrepreneurs. Advertising is sometimes sold to a customer at a reduced price when several months' exposure of the same ad are purchased at one time. If you are investigating successful ads, check back further than six or seven back issues. If you go back a year or more, however, and find identical ads being run, you can assume that they are paying for themselves. People would not pay to run the same ad over and over again, for long periods of time, if the ads were not working.

Ads are appearing in national magazines right now that I remember reading some 20 years ago. The ads have not changed much, and they are still in the same publications. These ads tell me two things. The target audience for the ads can be reached in the magazines where they show up year after year. And because the ads continue to run, they must be generating profits.

Two of the ads, in particular, that come to mind are not what you might think would endure the test of time. Someone advertises printed information on how to rid your garden and lawn of gophers. This ad doesn't sound like it would have a large appeal, but the ad has been in the same magazines for years and years. Another unlikely ad is one that offers information on employment in the Rocky Mountain states. Both of these ads are selling information, which is one of the leading products of mail-order merchants.

Going through old ads will tell you a lot. You can see what types of ads are successful, in terms of what is being offered, how the ads are worded, and where the ads are placed. This type of information is invaluable to you. It takes time to do the research, but this is the best way that I know of to refine your own marketing plan when you want to make it rich in mail order.

As you search through old ads, make notes about what you see. What is being offered? Do respondents have to call to order, or are they required to respond by mail? Is a fee charged for details on the ad, or are they free? Does the advertiser accept credit-card orders? Is an 800 number listed in the ad, or is the telephone number going to require a toll call for most respondents? Are the advertisers trying to make direct sales from their ads, or are they using a multiple-step marketing plan? We will discuss this procedure thoroughly in a later section. Is shipping and handling an added expense, or is it built into the cost of what is being offered for sale? Take plenty of notes and organize them carefully. What you find during your research is most likely what will make your idea win or lose.

Reviewing Your Homework

After going through many back issues of magazines, reviewing your homework can put you on the right track for success. Not only will you understand what ads work, you will see what types of products or services are suitable for successful mail-order sales. Printed matter is, by far, one of the most popular and profitable items to sell. But you will find mail-order ads for everything from fishing worms to pheasants. Quilts, woodworking kits, toys, games, haircare products, tobacco, and travel packages are all sold by mail. Mail-order madness is an open forum where you can market and sell almost anything.

You may already know exactly what you want to promote in your mail-order ads. If you don't, reading other successful ads is sure to give you ideas. In my opinion, you should avoid certain forms of mail-order business. Make sure that whatever you choose to do is legal. Many ads offer opportunity seekers a chance to open their own mail-order businesses as distributors. These situations can get sticky. If you see an ad in which a company wants you to sell its books, videotapes, or other products as a distributor, beware! If there was big profit in it, the parent company probably would be doing the sales itself. There are many traps and pitfalls in the mail-order maze, and we will talk about them as we cover the field.

As a part of your homework assignment, you should read books on the subject of mail-order businesses. There are plenty to choose from. I found that by reading several of these books, I was able to piece together tips from each one to make a good format for what will and what won't work. Of course, what works for me might not pay off for you. The more you can learn about the subject, the better off you will be.

Choosing Your Product

Choosing your product is an important early step in the development of your mail-order business. If you want to sell jumping beans, you can. But how much market is there for them? I remember an ad that used to sell sea horses, or something like that, and it was reported to be a huge moneymaker. It's hard to say what the next fad or gimmick will be. Pet rocks were hot for a while. Skateboards soared, crashed, and then rose from their own ashes to sell well yet again.

If you plan to sell typical merchandise, you must either manufacture it or find a wholesaler to work with. Selling information is easy. You just prepare pages of text and mail them out. You might be selling individual pages, brochures, or entire books. Some people sell bird eggs by mail. A number of mail-order ads promise the equivalent of mail-order brides and pen pals. The arena is wide open, so you can experiment with any legal sale that you wish to.

Mail-order sales are ideal for people who make and sell crafts. You can sell handcrafted birdhouses, rugs, stained-glass window hangings, photographs, T-shirts with slogans on them, or any number of other items. Keep in mind that heavy items cost more to ship, and fragile items can be broken in transportation. If you have several types of crafts to sell, a catalog is a good investment. Fill it with descriptive text and some black-and-white photos for maximum results.

In my opinion, it is difficult to compete in some markets. If you are not making your own products to sell, your profit margin will be lower. Buying from a wholesaler and selling to the public can work, but the profit percentage is lower. I recommend that you come up with something on your own that you can make. So many options are available that I can see no reason to pay a wholesaler for a product when there are good items that you can make and sell yourself.

Picking your products to sell is the easy part of a mail-order business. Selling them for a profit is what can be difficult. If you have done your homework, however, the odds are in your favor. You can even have your potential customers pay for your ads. Do you find this hard to believe? Well, let me tell you how I've done it in the past.

MAKE YOUR CUSTOMERS PAY FOR YOUR ADS

If you make your customers pay for your ads, your net profit will be higher. It may seem unreasonable to think that customers will pay for your advertising, but I've had them do it. Many years ago, I wanted to experiment with some advertising in photography magazines. The ad rates were high, but I had confidence in my plan. Basically, I was hoping to attract photographers who wanted to see their work published in magazines and newspapers. This is the ultimate dream of many photographers, and my intuition on the subject paid off. It worked this way:

I chose a premier photography magazine to run a test ad in. The cost of the advertisement was about $100. Keep in mind, this was more than nine years ago. My ad started off with the words, "Get Published Now." Then the ad went on to tell readers how I might be able to help them get their photos published. To receive complete details, respondents were asked to send $3 along with their names and addresses. I ran this ad for a few months, and I got about 100 responses each month. At $3 per respondent, I was receiving $300 a month. The ad cost me $100, so I was making a $200 profit before I ever sold anything.

Before we talk about what I sold and what the profit was in that regard, let's study what I've just told you. I had a net profit of about $200 a month from the ad, before I sold what I was advertising. This was with just one magazine. If I had placed five ads in five different magazines with the same results, I would have been making $1,000 a month, before any sales were made! Not too shabby, huh?

The sales package that I sent respondents required them to sign up with my agency. Frankly, I can't remember exactly what the charge was. However, I do remember that my average monthly profit from the deal was about $400, less mailing costs. In any event, you can see how something like this could be spread to a number of magazines to create a sizable monthly income, with very little effort on your part. Did I get anybody published? Yes, I did. By circulating the photos that were sent to me, I was able to find various buyers for the rights of the photos. Sales came mostly from magazines, but some businesses also purchased rights to the photos for advertising. My part in the publishing required an organized submission procedure, but not a lot of time. Even though I offered a money-back guarantee, I can't remember ever having anyone request a return of his or her money. It was a legitimate deal that worked for everyone.

All my mail-order dealings have revolved around either how-to information or some form of service, such as getting photographers published. I tried to market a newsletter for freelance writers and photographers with a mail-order approach and didn't make enough money to pursue the venture. While I didn't really lose much money, it was not lucrative enough to keep going.

Friends and acquaintances of mine have tried their hands in the mail-order maze with mixed results. Some have profited, while others have lost money. None of them have admitted to getting rich. But if you are looking for supplemental income, how much do you need? Is $200 a month from every magazine you advertise in enough? With 10 magazines, you would receive $2,000, after ad expenses. This, of course, is based on my personal experience. Your results may vary. The point is, you can make pretty significant side money without ever leaving the comfort of your home when you opt for a mail-order moonlighting routine. To recap:

- Keep your program simple.
- Ads should be informative, but concise.
- Weigh various types of media and their costs.
- Research the work of others.
- Evaluate your research findings closely.
- Get new ideas from the ads of others.
- Read books on the subject of mail order.
- Choose your products carefully.

ONE STEP, TWO STEPS, THREE STEPS

There are three basic approaches to selling with mail order. People in the business refer to them as steps. A one-step sale is when a sale is made directly from an advertisement. Having people request information about an ad and then getting them to buy from the information you send is a two-step sale. Three-step sales come after a prospect has responded to an ad and then received two informational mailings from you. The number of steps required to sell your product or service generally will depend on the price of what you are selling and how much space you need to illustrate its value.

Let's say that you sell small pamphlets of information. The price for them is about $8. You should be able to sell this type of product with a one-step approach. Advertising the product, the price, and ordering information in a classified advertising section of a magazine is probably all it will take to start getting money in your mailbox.

If you want to sell how-to manuals or cassette tape sets for $50 to $100, you should consider using more than one step to achieve your goal. Once the price of something exceeds $10 or $15, success with one-step sales, in classified ads, dwindles. A one-step pitch can be made in a large display ad, but these ads can cost thousands of dollars for just one appearance in a magazine.

A two-step sales program can be extremely effective. You advertise with small classified ads to attract attention. People contact you, by mail, telephone, or fax, for complete details. The details may be free, or you may charge a small fee for them. If the market you are working will pay a nominal fee for details, it's possible to pay for much of your advertising cost with the fees you take in.

The beauty of a two- or three-step sales approach is that you can provide prospects with as much information as you want. Space is limited in ads, even if they are full-page pitches. It is possible to give prospects too much information. Sales professionals believe that a confused mind always says "No." However, the more information you provide, if it is clear and well targeted, the more sales you are likely to get. Being clear and well targeted is especially important if you are selling a big-ticket item.

Running full-page ads in national magazines is a very expensive proposition. They can, and often do, work. But if you are not right on target with all aspects of your ad, you will lose a lot of money. First of all, does anyone want what you are selling? What is the most attractive, and profitable, price for your offering? Who is your market? Do you have any idea what type of information is most likely to trigger a buying response from your prospects? Before you invest in expensive advertising, you should have the answers to these questions. How can you get the answers? Use small, inexpensive ads to test the market. In doing this, you probably will use a two-step method. Let's look at an example.

Assume that I've come up with an idea for a safety product to be installed on recreational vehicles, such as motor homes and travel trailers. The piece is a simple, yet very effective, add-on that consumers can install themselves. This product protects people from getting burned on the outside exhaust of furnaces installed in the RVs.

My new invention will cost me about $7 to manufacture in small quantities. The price will go down if I can get into major production. Based on my guess of the market, I think I can sell the product for $29.95. This doesn't leave much profit if I spend big bucks for advertising. Maybe the product is worth $49.95, but I don't know. A test needs to be conducted. Here's how I will go about it.

Some magazines are natural targets for my advertising dollars. Any magazine that is read by RV owners is a good choice. But are other outdoor magazines viable considerations? They certainly could be. Sports people who read magazines pertaining to hunting and fishing might have campers. Readers of travel magazines also could own campers. A lot of potential markets exist, but I need to weed through them to find the best. To do this, I'm going to place affordable classified ads in several of them. The ads offer free details. Each ad is keyed with a code, so I know where my responses come from.

The key might be a department number, a different contact name, or an extension of my box number. For example, the ads that I run in RV magazines require correspondence to be addressed to R. E. Woodson. Ads in hunting magazines come to K. W. Woodson. My key for ads in travel magazines call for a contact person with the name A. A. Woodson. I could use department numbers, such as department 113, instead of the names. In some way, though, I need to know where the responses are coming from.

When mail starts to pour in, I assess where each piece is coming from. This tells me which magazines are working best for me. The next test will be in the text of my promotional pieces. I prepare three different pitch letters. If I get 90 responses from one magazine, I send a different presentation to each of the three 30-person groups. All of the prices are the same, only the descriptive sales pitch is different. This gives me a good handle on which pitch works best.

The sales price is my other main concern. To test between a price of $29.95 and $49.95, I do a mixed mailing to another group of prospects. One group is offered the low, introductory price of $29.95. The second group is asked to pay $49.95. When I get results from this test, I know what the percentages of success are with each price.

By the time my tests are completed, I can determine what is necessary to make an informed decision on a major ad campaign. The price of my product is defined. Knowing which magazines produce the most activity enables me to target the audience for my sales. And I have proven which pitch letters work best. At this time, I can consider running larger ads. It also makes sense for me to run more ads, based on my test findings. There still is some risk, but not nearly so much as there was before my test.

The effectiveness of my test is made possible with the two-step approach. I could accomplish the same goal with a three-step approach, but it doesn't seem necessary. A one-step approach, because of the price of my offering, doesn't seem feasible. Therefore, a two-step sales slant seems best. Do you agree? Think about it. Put yourself in the position of a prospect. How would you respond to different approaches? When you are working mail order, you have to rely on gut feelings and past experience. Some science may be involved, but a lot of the rewards come from trial-and-error experimentation.

Start to Finish

From start to finish, mail order is a high-risk, high profit–potential business. It appeals to a vast number of people, largely because it can be done from home and there is not much face-to-face contact with customers. I suspect that a lot of people fail at mail order. They probably read some of the get-rich-quick books on the subject and jump right into the game with all their working capital. Don't do this. Take your time. Test and test some more. Never risk more than you can afford to lose.

I remember reading advice in a mail-order book that explained how to leverage your ad costs so that the ads would not come due for payment until after money was rolling in from them. Even if you are able to postpone payment of your ads until after they are expected to work, there is no guarantee that you will earn a profit from the ads. In fact, you may not gross enough money to pay for the ads. Maybe I'm too conservative, but I strongly advise you not to place ads that you can't afford to pay for out of your moonlighting budget.

The mail-order maze, as I call it, is just that, a maze. Success or failure can be lurking in each corridor. There is more room for failure than success. To improve your odds, you must approach the mail-order market with a combination of confidence and respect. Fear is another name for respect in this case. You should be a little uneasy about your venture. If you lose all fear, you are much more likely to make mistakes, and they can be quite costly.

Certain key factors should be considered when starting a mail-order enterprise. We've talked about many of them, but there are others to think about. And even the ones that we have talked about need to become a part of your business plan for success. Let's run down a list of basics for you to apply to your mail-order operation.

Keep It Simple

The first rule of mail-order success is to keep your program simple. A complex approach is much more likely to fail than a simple one is. This advice pertains to everything from your advertising to your product or service offering. Even when doing a multistep sales pitch, you don't have enough of the prospect's attention or time to explain a complicated sale. Concentrate on keeping all your business components easy to comprehend.

Know Your Competition

One of the more important elements of creating a successful business of any type is knowing your competition. It can be easy to overcome competition if you know it exists and how it operates. But not having the information needed to beat your competitors can spell out a very short life span for your enterprise. Research what each and every competitor is offering and how the offerings are being made. Once you gather your facts, you can mount an attack that is likely to be successful.

Select a Product

Product choice is of paramount importance. This single step can make or break you as a mail-order entrepreneur. Many successful mail-order operators have sought their fortunes with printed matter. A good number of them have succeded, including myself. Books, pamphlets, and other printed matter are excellent choices for mail order. The product is durable, ships well, and often can be manufactured quickly. But you may not want to sell words.

Items made of fabric, such as quilts and rugs, are similar to printed products because they are durable and ship well. These handmade items, however, can be a bother to produce. You can't call your local printer and order an extra thousand quilts. Someone has to make them, and this can create a production nightmare. We will expand on production shortly.

Buying low and selling high is how some mail-order people make it big. If you have access to low-cost items that you can sell for a large profit, this can be a good field to enter. Make sure, however, that your suppliers have enough of the product to fill your orders. I remember a story about a man who was selling watches by mail order. He was flooded with orders and couldn't fill them, because his supplier ran out of watches.

Selling services by mail can present some problems, but it also can be very profitable. You might advertise workshops for an activity that you know very well. If you do so, people may book time in your training camp. This service is a solid approach to mail order, because you don't have to worry about shipping and supply.

Choose what you plan to sell carefully. Make sure that you can fulfill the orders of your customers. Keep in mind the losses you might suffer with broken shipments. Who's going to pay the shipping and handling charges? With heavy items, such as woodworking pieces or large rugs, the shipping costs can be quite substantial. Weigh all your options and examine all the risks before you make a decision on what to sell.

Inquiry Fees

Some argument exists about whether inquiry fees help you or hurt you in the mail-order business. A lot of people recommend offering free details, which result in more inquiries, but are the prospects as serious as those who would spend a few dollars for details? I don't think so. Most of my ad campaigns have required respondents to enclose some token amount of money, never more than $3 for complete details. By requiring some money for details, I accomplish two of my goals. First, I get some money to pay for my ad costs, even if the prospects don't buy my programs. Second, I qualify the prospects, to some extent, to see if they are willing to dip into their pockets.

A Numbers Game

Mail order is a numbers game. You can expect to sell only to a minute portion of the people who might respond to your advertising. Only a tiny fraction of the readership of a magazine is likely to respond to your ad. Out of the group that does respond, only a small percentage is likely to place orders. It's important to recognize this fact, but don't be intimidated by it. Even dealing in fractions, there is still a lot of money to be made in mail order.

Because the business depends on responses, you might find that your particular type of business does best by offering free details or a free catalog. Sending out this type of information gets expensive, but the idea is to make sales from what you send. I know that I've just told you how I require a payment for details, and this may sound like a contradiction. However, each type of business works differently. What works well for a worm farmer might not work at all for a publisher or for a toy maker. You have to test and refine your approach to hone it to maximum effectiveness.

Selling in Steps

Selling in steps is often the best way to make your mail-order business boom. Some products and services lend themselves to one-step sales. Most, however, require two-step sales, and some do best with three-step procedures. It is difficult to generalize a strategy around the number of steps required. In general, I'd say that if you are selling something that costs more than $20, use a multiple-step approach, although many advisers say that anything over $10 should not be marketed in a one-step approach.

Production

Production can be a big problem for you if your ads work quickly. Let's say that you are selling birdhouses and other forms of woodworking goods. Even if you have a good inventory on hand, your ads may pull more orders than you can fill. It's good to have a blossoming business, but it's terrible to waste advertising dollars and lose customers because you can't fill orders.

It's difficult to balance production with profits. If you have orders that you can't fill, you could hire an employee to help you. But to do so will complicate your business and eat into your profits on some sales. Is it worth it? Maybe—but maybe not. Think carefully about how you will produce what you sell in large quantities if you get lucky and hit the jackpot.

Shipping

Shipping costs on some items can be extremely high. Are you going to build this cost into your advertised price, or are you going to require your customers to pay extra for shipping? There are many advertisements in which you see the phrase, "plus shipping and handling." I assume, based on the repetition of these ads, that customers are willing to pay the cost of shipping. Personally, I prefer to include the cost in my sales price and play up the fact that shipping and handling fees are included. As a buyer, I'm more likely to respond to such an ad, so maybe that's why I sell the same way. You can structure your shipping costs any way that you like, but you must allow for the expense when planning your venture.

Fulfillment/Packaging

Fulfillment is a foul word in some circles. Book publishers whom I've known considered fulfillment to be one of the worst parts of the business. I disagree with this line of thinking. A heavy fulfillment schedule means that your sales efforts are working. To my way of thinking, this is good. However, plenty of people cringe at the thought of fulfillment. You should consider this aspect of your mail-order business.

My mail-order work has never required using large boxes or a warehouse. Because I've been selling services and printed matter, the fulfillment end of the job has been pretty simple for me. This may not be the case for you. Let's say that you are selling custom-crafted wind chimes. Delicate items require careful packing. You will need boxes, bubble wrap, and a place to keep your fragile inventory. A spare bedroom might work in the beginning, but if your business takes off, you may need more space and more help. Don't overlook the requirements of fulfillment when choosing a mail-order business.

Credit Cards

Being able to accept credit cards for purchases is a big advantage. It is difficult to set up a merchant account as a new business, and especially as a mail-order business. If you can arrange with your bank, or some other source, to gain the option of accepting credit cards, your business is more likely to succeed. I will warn you, however, getting merchant status is an uphill battle, so don't expect it to be easy. You may have to apply to dozens of providers before getting accepted into a program. And there is a very real possibility that you will not gain merchant status with any of them.

If you can't obtain your own merchant status, you can check into services where telephone answering and credit-card orders are performed for you. This type of service takes a bite out of your profit, but it may be worthwhile. I know that I've seen ads for services that will provide you with an 800 number for customers to call when telephone orders are taken with credit cards. Because I've never used one of these services, I can't elaborate on them. Check out the provider's references and proceed with caution. It's best to get your own merchant account, but one of the services could be beneficial if you are unable to set up your own account.

A mail-order business is a lot to bite off as a moonlighter. On the surface, the opportunity seems ideal, and it can be. But don't make the mistake of thinking that mail order is easy. It's not. Be prepared to devote a lot of time to research and testing if you expect to excel in the mad rush for mail-order buyers. You will have to deal with many competitors, but this is true of any lucrative field.

And mail-order can be quite lucrative. If you have the right idea, the right product, and a good plan, you might become the next mail-order millionaire.

To recap, always remember:

- Your customers may pay for your ad costs.
- One-step sales plans
- Two-step sales plans
- Three-step sales plans
- Key your ads.
- Track your results.
- Don't leverage your ad costs.
- Keep everything simple.
- Know your competition.
- Choose products carefully.
- Mail order is a numbers game.
- Production can be a problem.
- Shipping costs add up.
- Order fulfillment can be a headache.
- Being a credit-card merchant is a bonus.

12
COOKING UP PROFITS

D o you enjoy cooking? Are you a good cook? If so, you could be
ready to open your own moonlighting business as a cook or as
a caterer. There is big profit to be made in the food business.
Whether you operate a hot-dog cart or cater weddings, you can
make hundreds, perhaps thousands, of dollars a week in extra
money. Even if you are not an expert in the kitchen, you still can
cash in on the food craze. You don't have to slave over a hot stove
to roll in the cold cash on a weekend food event.

Some people, like my aunt, love to cook. Many of them never
sell their services as experts in a kitchen. But most of them could
in some form or fashion. When it comes to food, there are a lot of
ways to make money. Flipping hamburgers at the local fast-food
restaurant is one way, but it doesn't pay much. And I seriously doubt
if the job is much fun. There are, however, plenty of other opportunities for you in the food-preparation and food-service industry.
You can work from home, work for an employer, or work on location with a vending cart or truck. Let me tell you a few stories to
illustrate my point.

Shortly after graduation, I went to work in construction. About 10 each morning, a truck would pull up to the construction site where I worked. Dual horns would herald the arrival of what we fondly called the Roach Coach. It was a truck set up specifically for on-site food service. Construction workers would swarm out of the houses being built like hornets from a nest. Individual sales were not large, but they were numerous.

Around noon, the truck would return and the horns would sound again. Human bodies flocked to the food truck. This scene was repeated in the middle of the afternoon. Three times a day, the driver of the truck would deliver a variety of both hot- and cold-food options for workers to choose from. There were always long lines at the truck. I don't know how much money the owner of the business made, but if the activity on my project was duplicated throughout the day at other job sites, I can only imagine that the money made was substantial.

A man I know used to operate a hot-dog cart. He didn't own the business, but he handled all the money made from his location, which was an excellent one. The cart was set up in a very busy tourist-oriented town in Maine. According to the employee, it was not unusual to sell enough hot dogs in one day to gross $1,000. Judging from retail prices for hot dogs, buns, and condiments, this would translate into a profit of well over $700 a day, less labor expenses and sidewalk rent. Not a bad day's work.

Two men who used to work for me in construction liked to take a vending cart to fairs and carnivals in their off-hours. They sold french fries, hamburgers, hot dogs, and other event-type food. They told me that at the end of one summer season they had made more than $30,000 working with their cart. The men didn't travel more than 125 miles for any event, so they could have made a lot more if they had been willing to follow the circuit.

The markup on food is tremendous. Another friend of mine owned a restaurant for a while. He and I talked often about various business opportunities. During one of our discussions, he revealed to me the spread between his cost for food products and the menu prices. I was shocked to see how much markup was added to every item served in the restaurant. It was just incredible.

Not everyone is cut out to be a cook, but even if you're not, you can become involved in the highly profitable business of food preparation and service. You can be the brains behind the business and get a partner, employee, or independent contractor to perform the kitchen work.

Some types of food businesses work better for moonlighters than others do, especially if you want to take care of all aspects of the business yourself. Obviously, if you are working a full-time day job, you can't peddle hot dogs on the sidewalk or cruise construction sites for food sales during the day. Still, you can handle many types of food-related work in the evenings and on weekends. Let's look at some of your options on an individual basis. Some considerations for selling food are:

- Put your products on consignment in retail outlets.
- Become a weekend cart vendor.
- Deliver food to offices and construction sites.
- Cater special events.
- Offer food service for elderly customers.
- Bake and sell low-calorie food.
- Sell prepackaged, carry-in lunches.
- Create your own food events.
- Open a Kiddie Express business.
- Find your food niche.

LICENSING

Depending on where you will be working your food business, special licensing may be required. Health inspections are another consideration. Laws vary from place to place, so you will have to check with your local authorities to see what requirements your new enterprise must meet. Do this before you invest much time or money in a food business. Many localities offer reasonable licensing obligations, but some may be so strict that the business will not be worthwhile on a part-time basis. Check it out before you go too far.

WEDDING CAKES

A wedding cake is meant to be a once-in-a-lifetime goody. Because of the nature of weddings and the cakes that go with them, a lot of money often is paid for this type of cake. If you can bake a big cake and decorate it appropriately, you've got an easy opening to a good moonlighting business. There are a few glitches in the business, but the good points outweigh the bad ones.

Finding customers for a wedding-cake business is easy. Look in your local newspapers to find engagement announcements and wedding announcements. Clip them out and mail a brochure of your services to the people who plan to marry. You should be able to find their mailing addresses in either a regular telephone book or a cross-reference directory that lists telephone numbers and addresses. Some libraries carry cross-reference directories. You also can buy them directly from the companies that publish them. Either way, the reference or information desk at your local library will put you on the right track.

In addition to watching newspapers for announcements, you can post notices and hand out business cards. Placing advertisements in newspapers will work, but the cost might not be offset by new business. When you mail to people who are making announcements of engagement or marriage, you know you have live prospects. Talk to other business owners who cater to weddings. If they are in a business that is not competitive with yours, you probably can encourage them to make their customers aware of your services. In return, you can do the same for their businesses.

Before you do a lot of marketing, take some time to bake a few cakes. Keep track of your cost for ingredients, and pay attention to how much of your time is needed to make the cakes. Once the cakes are finished, take some quality photographs of them. Potential customers will need visual aids to decide what type of cake they want. You should make each kind of cake you plan to sell and take pictures of it. The pictures can be used in your business brochure and portfolio as well as in your album of selections.

Once you know what it costs to make a particular cake, you can assign a sales price to it. Don't note the price on the pictures in your album. Instead, print a price list that includes each cake and insert it at the back of the album. Putting prices on the individual pictures may have a bad influence on your sales when people are choosing the perfect cake for their weddings.

Most weddings take place on weekends. This is perfect for the moonlighter. You can create the cake during the week and deliver it on the day of the wedding. Allow yourself plenty of time. It's hard to imagine a scene where the wedding party is ready for cake and the cake has not yet been delivered. By taking advance orders and deposits, you can work at a comfortable pace and still make a lot of money moonlighting in your kitchen.

Supplier of Homemade Goods

Consider becoming a supplier of homemade goods. Restaurants and stores often feature homemade food items. The public loves to see something made special, and they will pay extra for it. You might make giant chocolate-chip cookies, wrap them in plastic wrap, and sell them at convenience stores, restaurants, and other outlets. Pies are another specialty that appeal to customers. Homemade jam can be a big hit. Whatever you enjoy making, people usually will buy.

The most difficult part of becoming a supplier is finding places to put your food on consignment. Of course, you could sell your products out of your home, if zoning, health, and licensing regulations will allow it. Putting food on consignment will mean that you have to discount the products for your buyers. You won't make so much money on a given item as you would selling it to consumers directly, but you should do a much higher volume of business.

When you are a wholesale supplier, you can build your route to suit your time requirements. Cook when you can and deliver when you have to. By keeping the shelves stocked at a number of stores, you should have a steady stream of cash flow rolling in. Don't overlook major grocery stores. They sometimes take on homemade goods as marketing experiments. Who knows, you might get lucky and strike it rich with a national campaign if the right people see and taste your products.

WEEKEND VENDOR

If you live in the right place, becoming a weekend vendor can be fun and profitable. You can prepare food during the week and sell it on weekends. To do this, you need permission to set up your cart or truck for sales. Contacting property owners usually will result in some form of negotiation. Expect to pay a lease fee for your vending spot. There are a number of sites where you might take your mobile food stand.

Flea markets attract a lot of interest. Some of these sales are huge. If you have a large flea market near your home, the parking lot could be an excellent place to sell food and refreshments. Renting a spot in the parking lot shouldn't be too expensive. If the market operates on a regular, weekend basis, you can become a fixture that repeat customers look for on every trip.

Construction workers, road workers, and other people often work on weekends. If you take your show on the road, you can become known as the weekend treat. Deliver special food items to the workers and watch the cash roll in. It helps to have a truck rigged for this type of work, but you can make do with a station wagon, van, or pickup truck. Put some coolers in the vehicle, fill them with food, drinks, and ice. Add magnetic signs and some type of signal horn, and you're in business.

Maybe you can set up your cart at weekend sporting events. Organizers of big events probably will not give you permission, but smaller ones, such as children's leagues, may welcome you. The key to success is finding places that attract people. Once you make your contacts, returning to the same sites week after week should produce good business.

EVENT CATERER

Have you ever considered becoming an event caterer? This is a business that lends itself well to moonlighters. And this venture doesn't require you to perform food preparation personally. Line up a list of independent contractors who can provide you with a variety of food items. Your job will be to sell the food and service to people planning the events. Your subcontractors will prepare and deliver the food. It is critical, however, to know that your suppliers are dependable. If anything goes wrong at the event, you are the one who will be blamed, and it will be your business that takes a beating in reputation.

Finding people to prepare food for you should be the easy part of this opportunity. Getting events to cater will be more difficult, until you become established. However, there is almost no overhead expense in operating this type of business. You don't have to buy commercial kitchen equipment or a truck. All you have to do is line up the work and oversee it.

Conventional advertising will drum up some business. A cheaper, and probably better, way of getting work is to network with other business owners who come into contact with people who plan events. Meeting planners, bridal consultants, florists, photographers, and people in similar services may be called when a person is planning a special event. Let these business owners know what you do and how to contact you. Get a grapevine of recommendations working for you, and you will have plenty of business with minimal expense.

To get started fast, you can do some small-scale events for nominal fees. For instance, you could offer to cater a Little League game as a charitable act. Cater a church picnic for the same reason. Explain to these customers that you are providing the services on an at-cost basis, charging nothing for the catering expertise and time. They pay only for the food. In this way you can test your food suppliers and start building your reputation rapidly. A few low-cost, high-exposure events can be all it takes to get you rolling on a steady diet of new business.

ELDERLY FOOD SERVICE

Elderly food service is an opportunity that may become a major moneymaker in the near future. It's already a good business, and it has potential to become very profitable. Get in on it now, before competition is too thick, and you can be in the driver's seat when the industry peaks.

When young people don't feel like cooking, they go to a restaurant. Many elderly folks can't afford this luxury. Even if they can, some of them don't have the physical ability to get out of their homes without a lot of fuss. The idea of having a pleasant person deliver a meal now and then can really appeal to these people. Hey, it would appeal to anyone!

You can take several approaches for your home-delivery service. Assuming that you work a full-time day job, making deliveries yourself can be difficult. It may be feasible to make arrangements with an independent contractor to deliver orders for you. Another possibility is to make your deliveries after your regular work is over. Make a cold lunch for your customer the night before. Prepare fast, warm meals when you get home from work. Set out on your route and deliver the meals. Your customer will have a hot supper and a bag lunch for the next day. You may be juggling a lot of work, and you may not feel up to the challenge. There is an alternative.

Offer your meals as weekend treats. In other words, run your delivery route only on weekends. Customers will come to look forward to the weekends with new enthusiasm, and the pressure will be off you. Consider offering a wide range of items that can be delivered on weekends and that last into the coming week. Pies, cakes, and some food dishes fit this bill. For example, a hearty pot of beef stew could be kept and reheated for multiple meals.

Tapping into the market for food service to the elderly could result in rich rewards. Getting customers is easy. Have some flyers printed and deliver them door-to-door. You can just leave them for residents to find, but a face-to-face meeting can go a long way in building a business relationship. Knock on some of the doors and introduce yourself and your services. Leave a menu with each resident. Before you know it, you may have more business than you can handle.

LOW-CALORIE BAKERY

By helping to reduce waistlines, you can increase the size of your bank account. Think about specializing in low-calorie foods that you can sell either directly or through consignment arrangements. Americans are seeking good-tasting, low-calorie foods more and more. If you can create recipes that are tasty with reduced calories, you could be walking the path to prosperity.

This business affords you an obvious way of making extra money, but there is another benefit that may not be so easy to see. Once you master a volume of recipes for your special foods, sell the recipes nationally. You can take out classified ads in newspapers and magazines to sell the recipes by mail. With a little luck, and a lot of persistence, you might be able to sell your cooking credentials to a major publisher and see your name on the cover of a cookbook.

Want some fast publicity for your specialized food? See if your local newspaper will consider letting you write a short column on the preparation of healthy foods. If the editor won't go for the idea, see if it might be possible for you to donate recipes periodically for publication as a public service in the newspaper. Ask the newspaper to give credit to you and your business for the donated recipes. Getting your name in the newspaper on a regular basis in this way is bound to be good for business.

CARRY-IN LUNCHES

Carry-in lunches can bag you a lot of cash if you are available to deliver them. People who work late shifts certainly can take advantage of this profitable moonlighting business. Your customers will be business owners and their employees. These people often have lunch delivered to them. After a while, all the typical deliveries become boring. If you come up with fresh ideas and great food, you can capture the customers and keep them.

To attract lunch business, all you have to do is drop off menus at various places of business. Require that all orders be placed by a certain time of day. This way, you will have time to prepare the food and get it delivered on time. It's very helpful to have a delivery person working with you, but it's not essential.

You will receive a certain amount of business in the lunch field simply by offering standard service. If you want to charge higher rates and become the talk of the town, mix in something special about your service. For example, you might make a delivery to a busy boardroom. Pack the food in a picnic basket, complete with checkered tablecloth. This little touch of personal service will boost your business reputation. Come up with similar gimmicks for all occasions. You could even get your business known for its various themes. This type of marketing makes the biggest winners.

SPORTSMAN'S PICKUP SERVICE

If you live in an area where hunting and fishing thrives, you can catch your share of cash early in the morning, before going to work. Prepare bag lunches and boxed breakfasts ahead of time to sell to anglers and hunters heading out for early excitement. Either place these on consignment in local convenience stores or sell them yourself from home. Serious sportsmen start their days before the sun comes up. Who knows, you may make more money before you go to work than you will at work.

ORGANIZE YOUR OWN EVENT

If you want to, you can organize your own event to cater. Have you ever been to an all-you-can-eat pancake breakfast? How about an outdoor barbecue where there were dozens of people? A crab feast? Or maybe a bean supper? People like to come to food events as social gatherings. These events give you an opportunity to make money and new friends at the same time.

To stage your own feast of fun, food, and entertainment, you will need a place to accommodate your customers, such as a large, open field, a recreational hall, or any other place that can handle a crowd. You may have to check with local fire codes to see what limitations your facility has pertaining to the number of people allowed to congregate in it.

Choose your meal and then advertise the big event in your local newspaper. Put notices up around town, and tell everyone you know about the great gathering that's coming up. You may need a few helpers to keep the food cooking and served. It's best if you can get reservations, but this is not always possible.

When you advertise your event, stress the social value of it. If children will be welcome, announce this fact. Weekends are ideal times for this type of function, so the job description fits well into the moonlighting category. Don't expect to get rich with your first attempt. You should make money right from the start, but more importantly, you want to build a list of customers who will come to your subsequent offerings.

When you sell tickets to the meal, ask people to write their names and addresses in a guest book. The book will be used to generate a mailing list that will make future gatherings more successful. By changing the theme and menu on a weekly basis, you can attract the same crowd over and over. Each event should grow in profit and popularity.

It's often possible to rent places that are set up for serving meals. Many of them already will have tables, chairs, and kitchens to work with. Local community centers are generally good places to consider indoor events. Schools are other possibilities, as are firehouses, churches, and other buildings that hold their own functions.

Running your own events can be risky. If a crowd doesn't turn out, you have a lot of food on your hands. A rented room could result in lost money. Advertising expenses can't be recovered. You must go into this opportunity knowing that it may not pay off. But if you hit the market right, the money earned can be very good, indeed.

KIDDIE EXPRESS

Setting up your own kiddie express is a great way to make extra money after work. You will need a truck or van to operate this business. As an alternative, you could use an enclosed utility trailer. Manufacturers make these trailers with swing-out doors that are perfect for a vending route. Ideally, your vehicle or trailer should be painted colorfully with images that will attract the attention of children. Bells are another good investment. If you've ever had an ice-cream truck come through your neighborhood, you know the image we are discussing.

Your customers normally will be in school while you are at work. When you get home and head out to local neighborhoods, the children should be excited to see you. Weekends give you entire days to ride around, selling your supplies. This is an excellent choice for moonlighting if you enjoy children.

Once you are ready to deliver your goods, you simply load your foods and hit the road. You will compete with ice-cream trucks, but your items will be different. Think about the types of food that are sold at fairs, carnivals, and ball games: candy apples, cotton candy, peanuts, popcorn, flavored ice, and so forth. Children love these goodies, and the profit from each sale has a staggering percentage of markup value. You can add to your food sales by selling balloons, posters, inexpensive toys, and other novelties.

If you want to put a different spin on this idea, you can set up your truck to offer healthy snacks that will appeal to the parents of your young customers. As long as the children are buying their snacks off a truck, they will be excited to get them. In either case, load up on plenty of liquid refreshments of all kinds.

You can dress up as a clown or wear regular street clothes when running your route. As a special treat for the children, you could wear different costumes on different days. If you live in an area where houses are situated close together, you can sell out of supplies quickly. Remember, though, to check local licensing requirements before you get started with this proposition.

FINDING YOUR FOOD NICHE

Finding your food niche should be easy now that you've read this chapter. There are, of course, additional opportunities that exist in the food business. The ones that you've just read about are more than enough to get you started. To recap, some ideas for food profits include:

- Bake wedding cakes.
- Make all types of homemade goodies.
- Bake and sell cookies.
- Pies can be good sellers.
- Bake beans and then promote a bean supper.
- Have a barbecue bash.
- Invite the public to a pancake breakfast.
- Sell box lunches.
- Use a vendor cart to sell your food.
- Deliver lunch to offices in picnic baskets.
- Concentrate on health foods.
- Hot dogs are always popular in vendor-cart situations.
- Popcorn, candy apples, and flavored ice can sell well.

See Chapter 14 for additional ideas. Feel free to add to the ideas and to revise them to suit your personal desires.

Is your future in food? It may well be. As you've seen, you don't have to be a gourmet cook to cash in on the food craze. All that is needed is a solid business plan and your personal attention. Of course, if you enjoy cooking, the options are even broader in this big, and growing, business field. Speaking of growing business fields, let's turn the page and go over Chapter 13 to find out how you can make money by being a savvy buyer.

13
Buying Low and Selling High

Buying low and selling high has long been one of the best ways to turn a profit. But it's easier said than done. How is it that some people just seem to fall into great deals? Sometimes it's luck, but it is often a developed skill that separates the winners from the losers. Knowing what to look for and having a good grasp of the current market is what it takes to be successful as a dealer. You may have this ability and not even realize it.

Do you have any hobbies? What do you enjoy doing most? Look at your answers to these two questions and you may find that you have a business opportunity right in front of you. Hobbies frequently can be converted to moneymaking careers. Photographers do it. Writers do it. Golfers sometimes do it. There is no reason why you can't consider turning your specialized knowledge and interest into a profitable venture.

Let me tell you a story about my earliest entrepreneurial experiences. When I was in school, I decided to become a supplier of fine candy and gum. Actually, all I did was go to the local five-and-dime store and stock up on the most popular bubblegum and candy. Fireballs were one of my bestsellers. At that time, I paid a penny for them and sold them for a nickel. Pretty good markup, huh? I was able to do this because I had the supply and it was in demand during school hours. Back then, my weekly allowance was 50 cents. During the course of a week, I made a lot more money selling goodies I bought at retail prices than I did mowing lawns or working odd jobs. I decided to be a dealer rather than a worker.

As I grew older, I developed a keen interest in guns, especially handguns. My love of the weapons was not aimed at commercial gains. I liked to buy them and shoot them. Rarely did I sell one. However, I made a deal of the decade, and it was no accident.

One summer day, I went to the local hardware store to look over the fishing baits. While in the store, I scrutinized the used guns in a glass case. There in front of me was an original, Walther PPK pistol, in .22 caliber. It was the "James Bond" gun, and I had to have it. I think the caliber used by 007 was a .380, but this one was close enough. The price tag was marked at $85. This surprised me, because the owner of the store was a knowledgeable gun person. The price seemed very low.

I rushed home and got my father to go with me to the hardware store. He had to fill out the papers and buy the gun; I wasn't old enough. It was also necessary for him to float me a loan for the purchase. Thankfully, he did. Well, I got the gun and enjoyed it for many years. It came with an original holster and an extra clip. Some years later, I needed money, so I sold the gun to my father for $250. Not a bad profit.

My dad kept the Walther for a year or so, and then he traded it on a new rifle. The gun shop where he made the deal gave him close to $600 for the pistol. I more than doubled my investment, and so did my father. These transactions occurred over time, but the concept remains. It is possible to buy low and sell high. And that is what we are going to cover in this chapter.

How About You?

How about you? What can you buy and sell to make money as a moonlighter? Antiques are one possibility. Stamps and baseball cards are others. Cars and trucks might fit the bill. To determine what your best avenue for success is, you must assess your interests. Maybe cameras will be your ticket to high profits. Believe it or not, garden vegetables could do the trick. A wealth of opportunities await the astute buyer who knows a value when it's seen. Some deals turn quickly, and others require patience—another factor you must consider when defining your business plan.

A few key factors contribute to great success in the buying and selling of goods. Knowing a good deal when it comes along is one of the most important elements of success. Being in a position to act quickly counts for a lot. Having an ability to resell what you buy is essential. With just these three elements, you can turn your hobby or special interest into a money machine. Let's look more closely at how you can do it.

Antiques

Antiques intrigue a lot of people. Some folks enjoy them for their age, while others make money selling them. It is possible to do both. I've known a few full-scale antique dealers. These people operate retail stores and run regular antique businesses. They seem to be doing all right financially. This is certainly one way to profit from antiques, but other ways may appeal more to you as a moonlighter.

A retired couple I knew owned a little shop that they opened only on weekends. During the week, this couple would go out scouting and buying. On weekends, they would sell the treasures that they had found in previous weeks. In this particular case, the store owners were retired, but they could just as easily have been modern moonlighters. You could go on buying sprees in the evenings and then run your shop on the weekends. However, the overhead of renting a shop can cut into your income considerably. This problem leads us to other alternatives.

If your home can be used as a place of business, you can set up shop there. Check local zoning requirements first. Putting antiques out on your lawn when you're home can be a good way to move them. If this isn't feasible, consider running classified ads in inexpensive newspapers and journals. Another option is placing your fantastic finds on consignment with some other antique dealer. Doing so chops away at your profit, but it affords your products good exposure and a high likelihood of sales success.

Becoming an antique dealer doesn't require a lot of cash. You will need money, or credit, to buy what you want to put into inventory. If you decide to advertise, you will need money for it. But you can do quite well with just consignment sales or for-sale signs. Your business may grow to a point where you want to invest in retail space. Maybe you can convert your garage into a shop, or you can always rent a place if the money coming in is good enough.

Here, again, are samples of what you can buy for resale:

- Antiques
- Stamps
- Coins
- Sports cards
- Guns
- Automobiles
- Cameras
- Garden vegetables
- Paintings
- Photographs

- T-shirts
- Mail-order food
- Toys

COLLECTIBLES

Collectibles are popular with many hobbyists. The range of potential products for this market is immense. Coins and stamps are well known as collectible. Elvis memorabilia is still hot, and comic books seem to draw a good crowd. Insulators from electrical poles fetch good prices, and milk cans are a perennial favorite. There may be no end to what people collect.

If you are interested in collectibles, you have an advantage over people who aren't in terms of moonlighting in the field. However, you don't have to be bitten by the collectibles bug to turn your interest to this lucrative business. Books are sold that describe a wide variety of collectibles. The publications generally include pictures and price ranges. Study enough of this material and you can become something of an expert. Then go out and find the items at bargain prices. Once you have purchased the collectibles, sell them for big bucks. It's not so hard as you might think.

Have you ever gone to yard sales or flea markets? A large number of people make a hobby out of doing just this. They go to one sale after another, mostly as a recreational activity. The things sold at these sales usually are cheap and often are not worth more than what you might pay for them. Occasionally, however, some terrific deals can be made, if you know what you are looking for.

I have a small collection of old MatchBox cars that I bought as a child. They have collector value, and these items are just the type of thing you might find at a yard sale or flea market. Barbie dolls are another good example. Believe it or not, people will pay outrageous prices for just the right doll, toy, or plate.

Study books on collectibles. Get to know what objects possess potential value. Then make the circuit of sales on the weekends and see if you can find any hidden treasures. Old books are a good example of what you might set your sights on. Sooner or later, you are going to stumble onto something valuable. In the sale, it will be cheap. But once you have it, and offer it to collectors, the price will be much higher. There are far too many opportunities in this field to detail them here. Spend some time in bookstores or libraries researching collectibles, and you will see what I mean.

CARS AND TRUCKS

Cars and trucks are big items, but they can bring big profits. Some people have a knack for making money with automobiles. If you like vehicles, this may be your best field. Do you have any skills for repair work or bodywork on cars and trucks? Do you have a garage to work in? If you answer affirmatively to these questions, you may be sitting on a moonlighting bonanza. Even if you are not mechanically inclined, you can use your mental skills to profit from vehicles by buying at auction prices and selling at book value. If you are mechanically inclined, you can make even more. The key elements to buying low and selling high are:

- Gaining product knowledge
- Learning to know a good deal when you see one
- Putting yourself in a position to act quickly
- Having an established market for what to buy

A friend of mine loves older cars and trucks. He's in the navy and works on vehicles as a hobby. This man is a wizard when it comes to restoring a vehicle. He finds the mechanical beasts for sale, in run-down condition, and buys them cheap. Then he restores them to a salable condition. All he has to do is park them near the road with for-sale signs in the windshields, and he makes money. This guy has sold several cars for hefty profits. Best of all, he enjoys the restoration and gets paid for it. Maybe you could do the same type of thing.

I know people who run backyard body shops. They buy wrecked vehicles for next to nothing and rebuild them to a respectable condition. Once the bodywork is completed, they sell them for good profits. These are mostly moonlighting projects. The people I know who do this generally have full-time jobs doing something else.

If you don't like to get your hands dirty or your knuckles busted on slipping wrenches, you might consider auctions. I bought a 1985 Dodge RamCharger from a guy about six years ago. The man operated his business out of his home. His garage was a workshop, and his lawn was a parking lot for used cars that he sells.

The vehicle I bought had been a service vehicle in the air force. It turned out that the man had bought it, along with other vehicles, at a surplus auction. He sold me the four-wheeler for considerably less than book value. I think the odometer had about 42,000 miles on it. It seemed to me that the military probably serviced the vehicle regularly, so I bought it. No, it wasn't camouflaged. Someone, probably the guy I bought it from, had given it a blue paint job and some detailing stripes. It was a good-looking truck.

I drive a new Jeep now, but the RamCharger is still in service. During my six years of ownership, the four-wheeler has needed very little attention. I got a good deal, and the man who sold it to me made a profit, probably a large one. If you have the credit or cash to buy vehicles at auctions, you can resell the automobiles for a good profit. Many of them don't require any extensive work before they can be sold to the public. You might, however, need a dealer's license to do this, so check with your local authorities. There is money to be made everywhere you look when buying cheap and selling high.

GARDEN VEGETABLES

Garden vegetables may seen like an unlikely profit center. Don't laugh, for there are greenbacks to be made with fresh fruits and vegetables. You can grow your own and sell them, or you can deal directly with farmers for a higher volume. Single sales won't amount to much, but when you have a high-traffic area to work, the cash can add up quickly.

During my life, I've lived in many parts of the country. I was born in Virginia. South Carolina was home for a while, and so was Colorado. Maine is where I've chosen to spend my most recent years, and probably my future ones. Regardless of where I've been, roadside vegetable stands and farmers' markets have flourished. People wouldn't set themselves up to sell garden goodies if they weren't making money at it.

Let's assume that you are an urban moonlighter. Let's further assume that you don't have the time, interest, or land to grow your own products. If you do have facilities for a large garden or greenhouse, consider cashing in on it. But for the sake of our example, we will work on a buying-and-selling premise.

Go to the country and talk with the farmers. Cut a deal with them to buy corn, beans, tomatoes, and other fresh produce in bulk for low prices. Most farmers will be happy to work with you. Once you have your suppliers, the rest is easy. Truck or trailer your inventory back to the city. Find a place where you can establish a site as your vending area. Check local regulations first, for you may need a vendor's license. Spend your off-hours sitting on the tailgate of your truck or minding your cart to sell the produce to the

people in your community. This kind of moonlighting is an easy
way to turn some quick cash with very little investment. I'll explain
how it is carried out in Maine.

People in Maine sell everything from blueberries to potatoes
on the side of the roads. Corn is another big attraction, as are rasp-
berries. The vendors put up wooden, stand-alone signs along the
roads. Tourists and locals see the signs and pull off the road to buy
the fresh fruits and vegetables. Pumpkins are big sellers in the fall.
Judging from the number of cars on the sides of the roads, this type
of business can be brisk and profitable.

Paintings, Photographs, and T-Shirts

Paintings, photographs, and T-shirts are some other items that you
can buy in bulk and sell for sizable profits. I'm sure that you've seen
roadside vendors selling large, velvetlike paintings. Certainly you've
seen people at booths in local malls where a variety of items were
being sold. A trip to the beach will show you how people sell T-
shirts and beach towels. There is money to be made here.

You can buy all types of products wholesale when you are willing to buy in bulk. If you have an outlet for selling the goods, your
profits can be high. Flea markets, fairs, malls, parking lots, and
roadside sites are all potential places of business. If you specialize,
you can go to events and set up shop. Let me give you an example.

My daughter enjoys taking her dogs to dog shows. Most of the
show sites we visit are casual. Generally, some vendors are around,
but competition in sales has been light at the shows we have
attended. If you were to load up with T-shirts that sported the pictures of favorite dog breeds and offer them for sale at the show, you
might do very well. The same goes for photos and paintings. I know
a place that will provide me with 500 8″ × 10″ black-and-white pho-

tographs from the same negative for only $80. This works out to 16 cents apiece. I've seen this size print selling for $35 at shows. Imagine that, a profit of more than $34 for each picture sold. Once you sell all your inventory, your profit is $17,000.

Mobile Kiddie Games

Mobile kiddie games are great ways to turn pennies into dollars. My wife receives catalogs from a company that sells a variety of party favors and children's novelties ridiculously cheap. We buy from it for birthday parties and other occasions. The types of products are similar to those that are offered as prizes at arcades and fairs. It's amazing to review the prices of the products.

Now consider this exclusive way to buy low and sell high with a unique angle. Have you ever seen anyone going from neighborhood to neighborhood with a mobile game station? I haven't. Ice-cream trucks drive through family neighborhoods, but that's about it. Why? Is it that nobody has thought to capitalize on a different aspect of the financial rewards? Maybe so.

Assuming that it is legal in your region, consider bringing games to children where they live. You can do this with a truck, a van, or a trailer. Find a wholesale supplier and buy a bunch of inexpensive, colorful prizes to give away. Based on the prices that I've seen, you could stock a considerable variety of items for less than $200.

Load your vehicle with portable games, such as a plastic, ring-toss game, some plastic ducks that will float in water, and so forth. If you need ideas for the games, just go to amusement parks or fairs. You can use anything from pin-the-tail-on-the-donkey to balloons and darts. Plenty of game ideas can be set up quickly and don't require a large cash investment.

Pull your rig into a neighborhood where children live and let a loudspeaker play some carnival music. If the area you are working has a playground, you've got a perfect place to conduct business. Even a cul-de-sac will work. Keep the music playing as you set up your temporary game station. Children will come see what you are doing out of curiosity.

You can charge children to play the games with the understanding that they are guaranteed to win a prize. Children love to win prizes. Let's say that you charge 50 cents per play and the prize you give away costs 5 cents. This doesn't seem like a lot of money, but the profit percentage is strong. Depending on your market, you might be able to charge more. Once you get a group of competitors, the change will start to add up.

This business suggestion can be carried out as described, or it could be blown to bigger proportions by taking your show to birthday parties, children's sporting events, and other gathering places where there are lots of children. Setting up a mobile game station might be just the right move to make.

FOOD BY MAIL

Food sold and shipped via mail is a bigger business than what you might realize. This is another great opportunity for the modern moonlighter. We live in a time when people frequently move from one place to another. Unlike the old days, when children stayed home on the farm, today's population is mobile. Jobs often require employees to transfer. There is a lot of moving going on. When this happens, people become separated from foods that they have come to enjoy. I know this from personal experience, because when I moved from Virginia to Maine, I lost access to some of my favorite foods. I live in a region where military influence is heavy. The people who serve our country are displaced regularly from the places that they think of fondly as home. When talking with local military people, I've found that they suffer, as I do, over the loss of favorite foods. This is your opportunity for making major money in the mail-order food business.

Maine is known and loved for its lobsters. A live Maine lobster is something of a delicacy. These crustaceans are shipped all over the world. Live Maine lobsters do sell well, both on the local level and with mail order.

If I wanted to, I think I could take out ads in specialty magazines and do a good business shipping lobsters to distant buyers. I know some people make small fortunes doing this. Ads are placed for the lobsters and orders come in. The people buy fresh, live lobsters from local fishermen. The per-pound price at the docks is much lower than it is in stores. Once the red, rubber-banded, clawed creatures are acquired, they are packed and shipped out to mail-order customers. A lobster that is bought locally can be sold for a huge profit.

Lobsters are not the only type of food source that can be sold in this manner. When I left the South, I longed for pork barbecue. For the longest time, I couldn't find it locally. My wife suffered a similar withdrawal from crabs that came from the Chesapeake Bay. Occasionally, we would order some of our old favorites by telephone. They would be shipped to us promptly, for a price. The same was true of Texarkana barbecue, which I believe to be the best in the world. Good old-fashioned catfish also could be ordered from Texas.

You may be wondering about people paying premium prices to get what is readily available to you. But there is a demand for a variety of regional products in different parts of the country. This demand extends right down to general, mass-market products that line the shelves in your local grocery store. To this day, my parents, who live in Virginia, have me ship them a special salad dressing that is available in Maine but not in Virginia.

All you have to do to make money with this idea is inventory your local resources and advertise in appropriate media for buyers. Look for items that are regional, such as genuine Smithfield ham, live Maine lobsters, or Louisiana crawfish. There will be people who want them. If you have easy access to the goods, you can advertise them in areas where availability is limited or nonexistent. This is a moneymaker that is easy to operate as a moonlighter.

BECOME A MARKETEER

If you like the idea of buying low and selling high, you're a natural for becoming a marketeer. Countless products can be bought and sold for a profit. Taking a traditional route, you must spend money to make money. However, there is a good way to reduce your cash needs and risks without giving up your ability to profit from the work of other people. Have I saved the best for last? Could be, so pay attention.

Up until now, we have been discussing basic buying and selling strategies. These strategies can work well, but they require that you buy before you can sell. What happens if you can't sell what you buy? You have a problem. The easy way to avoid this problem is to become a broker. Basically, you become a salesperson for a number of product providers. It's actually very easy.

Throughout this book, we have occasionally talked about selling on consignment. In our previous context, you were the person putting products on consignment. Suppose you become the one with whom others place consignment pieces? Whether you are dealing with a local retail facility, door-to-door sales, a roadside stand, or a mail-order business, this step can be lucrative.

As a moonlighter, you have limited time to devote to your business. To make the most money possible, you need to do what you do best. If this happens to be marketing and sales, you can profit by networking with a wide range of manufacturers and suppliers. Remember our example of selling fruits and vegetables? What would happen if you leased some space and opened your own farmers' market? You don't have to be a farmer to sell fresh food. If you control a good sales location, you can charge area farmers rent for selling in your space. This concept extends to flea markets.

I know of several locations where flea markets are held on a regular basis. The person who controls the sales space rents tables to anyone who is interested in participating. Think about this. You rent a roadside field or a parking lot that is not used on weekends. Let's say that your cost is $75 a weekend. The space is large enough to accommodate 100 tables. You rent the tables for $8 apiece, which is something of a bargain. If you get a full rental, you are looking at $1,600 a weekend, less your $75 rental fee for the landowner. Making in excess of $1,500 for two days as a promoter is not a bad deal. The landowner profits from unused space. People who rent your tables get the advantage of increased customer activity, because of the large number of diversified sales tables. You walk away with a big chunk of change for setting it all up. It's a win-win situation.

Maybe you prefer a more low-key type of moonlighting. Consider putting together a mail-order catalog. You can offer the products of as many local merchants as you care to contact. For example, your catalog could have a country theme. You might offer homemade preserves, handmade quilts, custom-crafted wood toys, and so forth. You line up the suppliers and compile the catalog. What you are advertising and selling is the catalog. Your independent suppliers are doing the hard work. When you get an order for a fancy birdhouse, you pocket the lion's share of the money and pass on the rest to your supplier.

Creating a catalog is not terribly difficult. If you do a black-and-white catalog, it's not even too expensive. Color pictures run up the cost considerably. Obtain quality pictures of every item your suppliers can provide you with. Select the ones that are most likely to be in demand and include them in your printed matter, along with descriptive captions. Other entries in the catalog can be pure text. This concept not only is easy, it can be extremely profitable. You must make sure, however, that your suppliers can keep up with the volume of your sales. Customers will be dismayed if their orders are not filled promptly. It helps, enormously, to be able to accept credit-card orders. An 800 number with an order desk is also a big advantage. You can rent this type of service on a monthly basis.

The concept behind becoming a marketeer is selling what other people make or provide to you for a profit. Many talented people have no ability when it comes to sales. You can help these people while helping yourself. Create a marketing network, and you could be rolling in the dough before you know it.

If you are blessed with a strong sales ability, there will be no stopping you. Any business owner should welcome additional sales. Show the owners how you can benefit their businesses, on a commission-only basis, and you will have a depth of products to sell that will be unequaled by anything that an individual might produce and sell.

The monster money in buying low and selling high is made by marketeers. The overhead for this type of business is very low. Printing costs and advertising are essentially the only draws on your bank account. You can start with cold calling and door knocking, which cost nothing except for your time. With refinements for your specific circumstances, getting into the business of selling business for other business owners is both easy, inexpensive, and potentially profitable.

14
OTHER MONEYMAKING OPPORTUNITIES

We've talked about many ways to get started as a modern moonlighter, but there are still other moneymaking opportunities to cover. Consider this chapter your idea chapter. Instead of going into a lot of details on how each moneymaker in this chapter might work, I'm going to provide you with a large group of possibilities to consider. Each business venture will be grouped in a specific category. For example, if you want to find some type of business that deals with animals, look for the heading that describes this field. Under each heading, there will be numerous suggestions on how you might profit from that area of interest. Among the host of moonlighting ideas are the following:

- Open your own advertising agency
- Repair appliances
- Clean cars
- Install auto accessories
- Clean carpets
- Become a clown
- Work as a personal trainer

- Raise exotic plants
- Become a decorating consultant
- Open a furniture stripping shop
- Make money with a black-and-white darkroom
- Refinish wood floors
- Build decks
- Become a personal organizer
- Build outdoor furniture
- Guide canoe trips
- Cut and sell firewood
- Refinish plumbing fixtures
- Learn taxidermy
- Paint lines in parking lots
- Offer services for swimming pool maintenance
- Be a trip promoter
- Turn your farm into a larger profit center
- Get into motor-home rentals
- Run a string of sporting camps

I would not be surprised to learn that you already have decided which moonlighting path to take. We have, after all, covered a lot of ground. But if you still aren't sure what you want to do, this chapter will be a catalyst to your imagination. There are so many business suggestions here that you are sure to find something that is right for you.

DIALING FOR DOLLARS

A telephone can be a powerful tool. If you have a pleasant telephone voice, you might make your moonlighting money without ever leaving your home. This section will offer plenty of tips on ways to go dialing for dollars. You can make money with your telephone by performing the following services for your clients:

- Cold calling potential customers
- Taking orders from customers
- Conducting telephone surveys
- Running an answering service

After-Hours Answering Service

Consider using your home as a base for an after-hours answering service. Your customers normally will be business owners. When you get home from work, change hats and start answering telephone calls for a wide range of customers. Businesses that employ office staff during the day often require the services of an answering service in the evening. You can start your moonlighting business on a small scale and grow with it as your customer base increases.

Cold Calling

Cold calling is a fact of life for many salespeople, and a lot of them hate this part of their career. You can solve their problem and yours at the same time. If you possess good communication skills and can accept rejection well, you have what it takes to be a cold caller. You don't have to do the selling. All your job requires is setting up appointments for the salespeople to pitch their products or services. Real estate brokers, insurance agents, and home-improvement companies are good places to look for customers. Plenty of other sales professions, of course, also use cold calling.

Order Taker

You could use your telephone to become an order taker. Contact local merchants and offer to take telephone orders for them after-hours. Explain how your service will enable the merchants to expand their sales by providing added hours in which their customers can place orders by telephone.

Telephone Surveys

Telephone surveys are conducted frequently to gather important marketing data. You can perform this type of work on your own and then sell the information you gather to various businesses. Another option is to offer your services to businesses for customized telephone surveys. You might conduct customer-satisfaction surveys for a car dealer, roofing surveys for a roofing company, or any number of other types of surveys.

CRAFTS

Crafts are popular both as hobbies and as moneymaking products. If you enjoy working with your hands, crafts can be a good field to consider getting into. From rugs to wreaths, there is money to be made. Craft moneymaking ideas including selling:

- Sand art
- Handmade birdhouses
- Cat climbers
- Handmade birdcages
- Handmade rugs
- Handmade lamps
- Handmade dolls

Sand Art

Sand art is a popular product in gift shops. If you like the idea of filling bottles with colored sand, you might be able to do what you enjoy and fill out your bank account at the same time. Depending on your circumstances, you might offer classes to teach people how to get beyond the basics in sand art. If you do this, be sure to have kits of bottles and sand available for sale.

Handmade Birdcages

Handmade birdcages could be your way of making it big as a moonlighter. With only a few tools and supplies, you can learn to build all types of birdcages. From fancy to simple, these items can be sold by mail, directly to customers, or on consignment. Sign and date each creation. Once word gets around, you may have more orders than you can fill.

Cat Climbers

Cat climbers are sold in pet stores at prices that could make you cringe. My wife saw a simple one just recently that was priced at $199. The climber consisted of two carpeted platforms, a carpeted tube, and some white birch logs. It costs very little to build this type of cat accessory, and if you go by price tags and inventory, the items must sell well and for a good profit.

Bird Feeders and Houses

Bird feeders and houses are good ways to make money from home. Build them in your spare time and place them on consignment in stores of all types. Create big ones, little ones, complex ones, and simple ones—all sell well. Want a hot tip? Build custom birdhouses that are fashioned after the home of your customer. Have a customer send you a picture of his or her home and build the birdhouse as a miniature of it.

Rugs

Rugs of all shapes and sizes can be sold for good prices. Create your own designs. Offer to make customized rugs for your customers. As with most other crafts, you should be able to get retailers to take your work on consignment. Display your work at craft fairs and sell it on the spot. Go prepared to take orders. Once people see your work, you may receive a lot of requests for rugs.

Unusual Lamps

Think about making unusual lamps at home and placing them for sale in gift shops. You might get a large glass jar, fill it with seashells, and then install a lamp kit on it. Combine some sand art with a lamp kit for a neat look. Use your creativity to come up with new and existing lamp designs.

Dolls

Dolls are always in demand. You can make your own dolls and create a custom collection. To beat the stiff competition you will face in this market, you have to offer something special. If you're lucky, your doll designs may be purchased by a toy company and become the next major line of dolls to rule the toy world.

Super Services

The service industry is full of opportunities for moonlighters. Many service businesses don't require you to carry an inventory or maintain a retail space. You often can work from your home to get your business going. As people become busier, the need for service providers expands. Take this opportunity to launch your moon-lighting business. You can moonlight in a service business by:

- Renting out yourself and your chain saw
- Offering a taxi service
- Becoming a credit counselor
- Providing elderly care
- Working as a personal shopper
- Conducting research
- Running a sharpening service
- Giving music lessons
- Doing housework

Chain Saws

Chain saws can be dangerous to work with and expensive to buy. If you own a good chain saw and can use it competently, you can offer your services with the saw to customers. Many people have occasional chain-saw work they would like to have done. Professional tree companies charge very high rates. While you might not want to cut down large trees for a living, you can do quite well working part-time with your chain saw.

Taxi Service

Opening your own taxi service can be very profitable. You can offer your services as a general taxi or you can specialize in working with elderly customers. Older people often are afraid to go out alone in the evenings. As a special taxi and escort, you can provide both transportation and a sense of security for your customers. Check into the licensing requirements for this type of business before you invest in it.

Credit Counselor

The need for credit counselors continues to grow. More and more people need help managing their money. It's surprising how many people don't know how to maintain accurate records in their own checkbooks. If you have the right skills to help people manage their spending habits, this could be a profitable part-time business with a lot of growth potential.

Evening Elderly Care

Providing evening elderly care is a good opportunity to consider. Many people have aging parents living with them. While care might be provided during the day on a regular basis, it can be difficult to find suitable people to spend time with elderly people at night and on the weekends. If a couple is taking care of a parent and they want to go out to dinner and to a movie, they need someone to watch over their loved one. You could be the person to provide the service.

Personal Shopper

You may laugh, but many people will pay you to be their personal shopper. Some people hate to shop. Whether buying groceries or holiday gifts or a wardrobe, there is a demand for personal shoppers. This is a job that you should be able to do after normal working hours, so it works well for moonlighters.

Researcher

If you have a computer or are willing to spend many hours a week in your local library, you can become a paid researcher. College students will hire you to research all types of information. People will pay you to track the genealogy of their family. Companies will ask you to research a variety of information. This is good work for a person who wants to minimize customer contact and work independently.

Sharpening Service

If you are good at sharpening knives, blades, and tools, you can open your own sharpening service. Saws, knives, lawn-mower blades, drill bits, axes, and so forth all need to be sharpened periodically. This is a service you can perform in your basement or garage. There is little overhead expense, and the pay is good. Get work by advising store managers at hardware stores, lawn-and-garden stores, and similar places of business of your services.

Music Lessons

If you are talented with a musical instrument, you can offer your services as an in-home music teacher. The fact that you come to the customer's home is appealing, and the one-on-one instruction is something that most people will pay extra for.

Housework

With the busy schedules most people keep to stay one step in front of the bill collectors, housework often is ignored. If you don't mind domestic duties, you can earn some good money by doing housework for your neighbors. Washing dishes and clothes is part of the job. Picking up after children may be in your job description. By helping working parents keep their homes clean while they spend quality time with their children, you can make a good part-time income.

CHILDREN

Children account for a large percentage of this country's population. They create an industry that is filled with opportunities for entrepreneurs. If you like children, you can enjoy yourself and beef up your bank account at the same time. Moonlighting opportunities that are centered around children are:

- Planning parties
- Baby-sitting
- Giving guided tours of zoos and museums
- Becoming known as "Mom's Taxi"
- Providing instructional services in specialized fields
- Sharing your knowledge with weekend workshops

Party Planner

Become a party planner in your spare time. Make arrangements for birthday parties and other functions for children. You handle all the details, so the parents can relax and know that their children will have a great time. Establish contact with several places where parties can be held. Find wholesalers who will sell you party supplies, decorations, and novelties at low prices. Once you get a customer, you are likely to enjoy repeat business year after year.

Baby-Sitting

Baby-sitting is not just for teenagers anymore. With the high demand and low supply of mature baby-sitters, you can make a good chunk of change for spending an evening with someone else's children. Parents will gladly pay more for a mature adult to watch their children. Just the fact that the sitter doesn't have to be picked up and dropped off is reason enough to pay more. You won't get rich as a baby-sitter, but it can be rewarding work in more ways than one.

Tour Guide

You can become a tour guide for children. Whether you are visiting a zoo or a museum, you can provide adult supervision for children who want to see the sights. Make arrangements for parents to get the children to the place where the tour will take place. Your job will be to keep the children together, show them the sights, and answer their questions. Parents can go shopping or out to eat while you provide the equivalent of an educational baby-sitting service.

Mom's Taxi

Parents with older children are constantly faced with transportation problems. One child has a soccer game on the east end of town at the same time another child has music lessons on the west side. Active children enroll in a number of activities that require transportation. You can cash in on this by setting yourself up as a mom's taxi. Once you build up a good reputation, you will have more work than you can keep up with.

Instructional Services

If you are an expert at something, you can offer yourself to parents for instructional services. You might teach a child to ski or swim. Maybe you can provide pointers on how to bat a baseball better. Whatever special skills you have that pertain to children can be harnessed and sold to parents. The training can be performed on location, so you don't need a special facility to work from.

Weekend Workshops

Parents often long for a weekend alone, which is too often a fantasy that can't be realized. However, you can make the dreams of parents come true when you offer weekend workshops for children. Parents deliver their children to you on either a Friday evening or a Saturday morning. The children spend the night, or nights, at the workshop, giving parents a weekend to themselves, and the children fun at your workshop. Make lodging arrangements at campgrounds, lodges, or other suitable locations. Depending on the number of children you're in charge of, you might want a helper to work with you. Take the children on nature walks. Introduce them to bird-watching. Show them how to make plaster casts of animal tracks. Use your personal abilities as a guide for them. The key is letting the parents have the weekend off, for which you can charge a handsome fee.

ANIMALS

Animals are pets, food, and sport for some people. It doesn't matter if you live in a city or out on a farm. The way you approach the businesses will vary with location, but there are plenty of moneymaking ideas to go around in either location. You can work with animals by:

- Training them
- Exercising them
- Grooming them
- Pet-sitting
- Working as a professional handler
- Becoming a dog or cat breeder
- Raising game birds
- Worm farming

- Breeding small animals
- Opening a petting zoo of your own

Trainer

If you are good with animals, such as dogs, you might consider becoming a trainer. You can train for obedience or for hunting. Trainers can command large fees for their services. People often don't have the time, ability, or patience to train their own dogs. If you can do the job, you can make serious money.

Exerciser

Offer to take animals out after normal working hours to exercise them. People who live in urban environments can't just turn their pets loose and let them run. Someone has to take the animals out for walks. This someone could be you.

Groomer

Grooming cats and dogs is big business. If you enjoy working with these animals and know how to keep them looking good, you can make major money in your spare time. Repeat business is almost a given in this situation. You will need to buy some equipment, but the total investment will not be very much. You can work on location, in your garage, in your basement, or even in a spare bedroom. This is a part-time business opportunity that could quickly produce full-time income.

Pet-Sitter

Pet-sitting is a business that continues to grow. When people are away from their homes, they need someone to feed, provide water, and care for their pets. This is something that you can do as a moonlighter. There's pretty good money in this when you work, but it is difficult to maintain a full schedule of work.

Dog Handler

People who own show dogs often hire professional handlers to work with their dogs during a show. This is not a job that just anyone can do. If you're good with dogs and are willing to invest some time in training yourself as a handler, however, the payoff can be generous.

Breeder

Breeding cats or dogs can be a profitable venture. This is a job that requires more time than you may think. Be prepared to spend a lot of your off-hours working with your stock. In return, you can earn substantial money if you are working with popular breeds of dogs and cats. It also helps to be able to accept major credit cards for purchases.

Game Birds

Game birds, such as pheasants and quail, can make you a wealthy moonlighter if you have the proper provisions for them. I raise pheasants now and will be expanding into quail. These birds require very little care and can be sold to sporting clubs, dog trainers, and fine restaurants. Start-up costs are low, and the profit potential is high. You should, however, have some rural space to use for your bird containment.

Worm Farming

Worm farming may sound like a strange business to consider, but it can be very profitable. You can buy worms in bulk very inexpensively. They can be kept and bred in ice coolers, aquariums, your backyard, or almost anywhere. The worms require very little attention and can help do away with your garbage. Once they mature, you can sell them to stores for resale as fish bait. This is a low-impact, inexpensive moonlighting venture to consider.

As an extension to your bait business, you might consider crickets and minnows. Minnows require aerated tanks or ponds to live in, but they reproduce in large numbers. Unlike worms, minnows are more difficult to keep alive and healthy during raising and shipping, but they fetch a pretty penny at the bait counter. Crickets multiply very quickly, and they can be sold as fish bait or as food for some pets, such as iguanas.

Furry Critters

Furry critters, such as Angora rabbits, hamsters, rats (not the city type), and guinea pigs, can be bred for profit. Your markets will include consumers and pet stores. Colleges and laboratories offer other outlets for bulk sales if you don't have a problem with your critters being used for experiments. If you have the space to set up pens, you can create a good income by breeding all types of animals.

A Petting Zoo

If you have the space, the time, and a good location, you can start your own petting zoo. People often buy animals and then need to get rid of them. You can acquire goats, chickens, pigs, and a variety of other animals at very low cost. Sometimes they are free for the taking. Get these animals and provide them with a secure home where they can put smiles on the faces of children. Charge admission to your weekend petting zoo and enjoy your animals and your cash. I strongly recommend that you consider getting liability insurance before you open your gates.

MORE, MORE, MORE

Have you found the right moonlighting venture for yourself yet? Do you need more ideas? Well, I'll give you more. Because of the confines of space, I can't give you a large quantity with a lot of descriptions. So I'll plant the seeds and let you grow the details. Prepare yourself for a long list of moneymaking potential.

Advertising Agency

Open your own advertising agency. Many of your clients will be easier to reach in the evenings than during the day. Your customers will be small-business owners who work during the day and perform office duties in the evenings and on weekends.

Appliance Repair

Take a course in appliance repair and offer after-hours service calls. Homeowners will love the fact that they don't have to take time off from work to be home when you come to repair their major appliances.

Clean Cars

Clean cars as your moonlighting enterprise. Auto detailing has become very popular, and this is work that you can do almost anytime. The money made can stagger your imagination.

Install Auto Accessories

If you have the ability to install auto accessories, such as radios and fog lights, you've got an income opportunity at your fingertips. Advertise your services at local auto-parts stores.

Clean Carpets

Buy or rent carpet-cleaning equipment and hire yourself out to clean carpets in the evenings and on weekends. Start by renting the equipment to test your market. If the work is available in a suitable quantity, invest in your own equipment.

Work with Leather

If you can work with leather, you can make money hand over fist. Create belts, vests, and other leather items that can be sold at craft shows and placed on consignment in stores.

Become a Clown

Become a clown and rent yourself out for children's parties. Dress up in various costumes and deliver singing telegrams, balloons, and other greetings.

Personal Trainer

If you are a fitness fanatic, you probably can sell your services as a personal trainer. Just talking to people around the gym where you work out should get you enough business to start referrals coming in.

Exotic Plants

Build a small greenhouse in your backyard and grow exotic plants. Your markets will be business owners, nurseries, and consumers.

Decorating Consultant

If you have a flair for decorating, offer your services as a decorating consultant. Make arrangements with wholesale suppliers so that you can sell wall coverings and similar products to the customers you consult with.

Be a Furniture Stripper

If you have a basement or garage to work in, you can be a furniture stripper. There is a fairly constant demand for this work, and it is something that you can do at your own pace.

Custom Black-and-White Prints

Set up your own black-and-white darkroom for less than $200 and offer custom prints from your customers' negatives. There are plenty of one-hour, color photo shops, but black-and-white labs are not so easy to come by.

Refinish Wood Floors

Refinish wood floors in your spare time. You can rent the equipment you need when your business is sprouting. Once it is in full bloom, buy your own equipment.

Organizer

If you have good organizational skills, you can become a part-time, professional organizer. Get paid to organize the offices of executives and the kitchens of busy people. This may not sound like a viable business, but it is one that is growing quickly.

Build Decks

If you can build decks, you can make big money in your off-hours. Deck construction is a booming business, and the profit margin for the work is large. A skilled carpenter can build a deck in a day or two, once the foundation is in, and pocket well over $1,000.

Outdoor Furniture

If you have good road exposure and a truck or a trailer, consider building outdoor furniture, such as picnic tables, chairs, and benches. This work can be extremely profitable, even though it tends to be seasonal.

Canoe Trips

If you live near a river where good canoeing is possible, think about renting canoes and running a shuttle service on the weekends. Drop off your customers up the river and pick them up downstream.

Firewood

Cutting and stacking firewood is physical work, but it can pay big dividends. In Maine, where wood is plentiful, a cord of seasoned hardwood sells for about $125. If you have access to free or cheap woodlots, this can be a very profitable business. People who live in the city and buy wood by the bundle, rather than by the truckload, will really boost your earnings. Many landowners will allow you to cut and haul deadwood for free. Some may even pay you to clear their land and let you keep the wood as a bonus.

Taxidermy

Taxidermy is a skill that you can learn through correspondence courses. Once you are prepared to mount fish, birds, and animals, you can turn your spare time into a lot of spare cash. Prices for mounting trophy fish and animals are astronomical. Once you start stuffing animals for sports people, you will have plenty of greenbacks to stuff your mattress with.

Refinish Plumbing Fixtures

With a nominal investment in time and money, you can refinish plumbing fixtures for a profit. Bathtubs will be your main source of income, but sinks, showers, and toilets will also generate cash.

Paint the Stripes

Paint the stripes in parking lots for commercial customers. This business is ideal for a moonlighter. Merchants don't want their parking lots blocked off during business hours, so you can paint the parking lines in the evenings. Start-up costs can be kept affordable, and your customers should come back to you time and time again.

Swimming Pools

Swimming pools require a lot of maintenance. If you live in an area where pools are prolific, you can turn your off-hours into cash by caring for pools. People who own pools usually can afford to pay a pretty price for keeping their water clean and inviting.

Trip Promoter

If you have a special hobby or a love that you are experienced with, you might be able to turn a dollar with it as a trip promoter. For example, you might lead an expedition of metal detectorists on a weekend hunt for treasure. You could give hiking tours of your local mountains. There is no end to what a creative entrepreneur can do in this field of endeavor.

Farm Fun

If you live on a farm, you can get people to pay you to do your work for you. It's true, people will pay to have fun on your farm. What you consider daily chores will be a treat to some people. Milking a cow, tossing bales of hay, or bringing in the corn all can be great fun for people who have never experienced farming. Don't overlook this opportunity if you have the proper facilities.

Motor-Home Rentals

Motor-home rentals are expensive. If you've ever had a desire to own a land yacht, this is one way to make it pay for itself, and then some. Buy a used motor home and rent it to people for trips. Make sure you have a good insurance policy and a damage deposit from the lessors. You could turn over several hundred dollars a week doing this.

Rustic Camps

Rustic camps can produce a lot of money for you and not require much of your time. Let's say that you live in the Washington, D.C., area. You buy a piece of land with a rustic cabin on it in the Blue Ridge Mountains only a couple of hours from the big city. Rent the cabin out by the week or by the weekend. There's not much that people can hurt, and city dwellers will jump at the opportunity to commune with nature. Again, you can see hundreds of dollars a week in profits from this type of venture.

ON AND ON

We could go on and on with ideas for moonlighting. There is no end to the ways to make money in your spare time. All you have to do is pick a path to pursue. Some cost more than others to try, but you can get started in hundreds of different types of businesses without much money.

BEATING THE BURNOUT

FOUR

15
THE SAME OLD THING

Doing the same old thing day in and day out can become very boring. Even if you start out enjoying what you're doing, you probably will tire of it after a while. This is a trap that many moonlighters fall into. They choose to moonlight doing the same type of work that they do at their regular jobs. Before long, they burn out on their job and in their moonlighting. Don't let this happen to you. Choose a moonlighting career that is different and exciting. You will be spending many hours working your second job, so it should be one that you can have some fun with.

Another problem that moonlighters often suffer from is lost personal time. Anyone who starts a business learns quickly that the time demands can be extreme. Moonlighters who have families find quickly that it is very difficult to find enough time for work and play. Don't let your second income cost you your family life and personal time.

Addiction is common among moonlighters. Seeing a bank account grow as quickly as it can from moonlighting can be all it takes to turn you into a workaholic. It's not easy to stop when you are making a lot of money. Sometimes it's not just the cash. The reason for getting hooked on work can be the result of wanting to build your moonlighting venture into a full-time business. Whatever the reason, the result is the same. All work and no play is not good.

As you move into moonlighting, you will find that there are many factors to be cautious of. Having been in business for so long myself, I can help you avoid many of the risks and problems associated with moonlighting and owning your own business. To get started, let's flesh out the three problems I've just mentioned to you.

BREAK NEW GROUND

Try to break new ground with your moonlighting work. If you are a hairstylist by day, sell real estate in the evening. The people whose hair you work with each day are all potential prospects for your sales efforts in real estate. Whenever possible, do something different in your after-hours work.

When I wanted to start my plumbing company, I raised the money by moonlighting. I worked all day as a plumber for an employer, and then I worked all night for myself as a plumber. There were times when I would clock more than 16 hours of nonstop plumbing. This pace is too much to stand for long. I did it because I wanted to establish a plumbing business. If I had been looking for extra money only, however, I probably would have been a part-time photographer instead of a part-time plumber.

One reason moonlighters do the same thing in their part-time business as they do in their full-time business is that they feel safer. It's also frequently easier to get business and make more money when you do something that you are already familiar with. But making a change and pursuing a dream can be a lot more fun. Because you will be maintaining the security of your job, try moonlighting with something that you will enjoy.

Make Time for Yourself

If you want to have a personal life and a moonlighting career, you must make time for yourself. Otherwise, you will find yourself working all the time. It's difficult to turn off the moonlighting thoughts. Being in business for yourself is very different from working a regular job. You probably can leave your day job right at quitting time without feeling one bit bad about it. This may not be the case when you start your own business.

To assure yourself of some quality time, you have to make rules that you are willing to work with. Maybe your rule will be that you take one hour off each day before you start moonlighting, and you only moonlight for two hours a night and four hours on weekend days. Another way might be to give yourself two nights a week off with no moonlighting activity. Maybe you will work all day on Saturday and take every Sunday off. How you divide up your time is up to you. The important thing is that you make provisions to give yourself a break.

Don't Get Greedy

Greed can get the best of you. Going too fast and too hard can result in a short trip. The slow, steady path is often the best one. Forcing your new business to grow too quickly can result in total failure. Pace yourself, and let your business grow at a comfortable rate.

My wife used to call me a workaholic, and I guess she was right. To this day, it's hard for me to stop working. Even when I'm supposed to be off and on my own time, I'm thinking about business. This is not healthy. I know it, but I can't seem to help it. Over the years, I've gotten much better about taking time off to look at life as something other than a business opportunity. While I can't say that I'm cured, at least I've made great progress in turning off the business valve. My drive has not been greed, it has been a desire to be successful. Only recently have I started to understand that success is not always measured with money.

There is a very high risk that you can become consumed by your business. You can say it won't happen. Once you get started, though, you may find yourself caught up in the jazz of wheeling and dealing. It truly can be addictive, so keep yourself in tune to what you're doing. Don't let your business be your life.

Don't Gamble More than You Can Afford to Lose

When you start your business, don't gamble more than you can afford to lose. This is an important rule. You may be tempted to risk more money than you can really afford to. Many moonlighting ventures don't require a lot of start-up capital, but some do. Pick a business that fits your budget.

People who start their own businesses sometimes make many financial mistakes. If you make too many, too soon, you will be out of business in a hurry. Take your time. Test your market. Build your business carefully. Avoid high risks. Wanting to see your business take off and soar is natural. Having the patience to see that it does is something that has to be learned. Let me give you a quick example to consider.

Assume that you are going to start moonlighting as a bridal consultant and wedding photographer. This is a business that doesn't require much overhead, and the start-up cost is manageable. Still, there is a way to sink yourself quickly, if you are not careful. Once you are ready to do business, you need customers. This is where you are most likely to make costly mistakes.

The safe way to build your business is to check newspapers for engagement and wedding announcements, contacting the people who plan to marry. Another safe way to gain momentum is to place notices and business cards in as many stores and shops as you can. You should also talk to any business owner who is involved with weddings. Make him or her aware of your services. Because you are a bridal consultant, the business owners should send business your way, knowing that you will likely produce customers for them. If you take this approach, there is very little risk to your new venture. Most of your money stays in your pocket, and business will build over time.

If you become impatient and start advertising heavily for new business, you could lose your life savings. Running large print ads and television commercials is very expensive. Good advertising often pays for itself, but sometimes it doesn't. If you spend thousands of dollars on ads that don't generate business, your money is gone and you still don't have any weddings to work with. This is a sad state to find yourself in.

Going into business is always a gamble. There is always some risk that you will not make money and that you may lose money. The degree of risk depends on many factors. Your experience is one key to risk reduction. Different types of businesses carry different types of risk. By assessing your circumstances and moving in small steps, you can limit your risk to a level that you can live with. Learn to do this, and you should prosper.

SEPARATE YOURSELF

Separate yourself from your work with mental and physical barriers. Doing so is especially important if you conduct your moonlighting from home. It's fine to work from your dining-room table, but it can be difficult to enjoy a relaxing meal in your office. Think about it. If your dining room is your office, where can you eat without thinking about business? To avoid burnout, you have to find ways to keep your business life in perspective.

If you will be working from home, try to give yourself a work space that does not double as living space. This much space may not be possible, but try. If you get creative, you can find ways to separate your work area. Buy dividers like the ones used in large offices to create cubicles. If you prefer, hang an old bedsheet from a ceiling to provide a separation. Of course, don't do this if customers will be coming to your in-home office.

It's very difficult to walk past your workstation without having your mind click onto business thoughts. If you can close a door and leave your work behind when you go into the rest of your house, it will be much easier to enjoy a normal life. As a moonlighter, you work day and night, but you don't have to work every waking hour.

FIND A BALANCE

Find a balance between work and play that is comfortable for you. Some people have personalities that drive them to stay busy all the time. If you are one of these people, moonlighting is an excellent outlet for your energy. Not only will you avoid watching television shows for entertainment, you'll be making money while keeping busy.

Most people need some amount of private time, time that is different from personal time. Spending time with your spouse or children can be considered personal time. Private time is when you are alone. Certain people don't like to be by themselves. Personally, I cherish my private time. Whether I'm reading a book, walking in the woods watching hawks soar, or playing with my dog, private time revitalizes me.

With my heavy work schedule, time is difficult to come by. What little of it I get usually is spent as personal time—most often with my children. My wife and I enjoy an hour together now and then, but the children keep us busy most of the time. Occasionally, I take a "Daddy Time-Out" and go off to be by myself for a while. At other times, I do child duty and let my wife escape to private moments.

I can be walking through the woods with my dog and be hit by a brilliant business idea. Even though I'm on private time, my mind doesn't shut out business altogether. It might be nice if it did, but it doesn't. Hopefully, you will be able to totally relax during your personal and private time.

In my opinion, stepping away from business now and then is essential to the success of your business. If you stay in the trenches day and night, you lose sight of things. Perspective is lost. You are concentrating so hard on what you are doing that you are not getting fresh ideas. Taking some time off will help you to avoid burnout and will very likely fuel your creative fires to come up with bigger and better business options.

COMPETITION

Competition is a fact of life in almost any business. If you don't have any competition, there is probably very little demand for what you're doing. Where there is demand, there will be people providing a supply. Business owners look at competition in different ways. Some owners want to blow out their competition completely. Resentment can run high between competitors. A few smart business owners accept their competition and work with it instead of against it. Let me remind you of something I wrote earlier in this book.

Do you remember the moonlighting opportunity where you load up a truck with cotton candy and other types of junk food? If you recall, I said that you might run into competition with ice-cream vendors, but that they would not be direct competition.

This is what I mean when I say that you work with your competitors. People who buy ice cream probably aren't looking to buy candy apples or cotton candy at the same time. They might buy ice cream today and cotton candy tomorrow. You and the ice-cream vendor are working the same crowd, but you are not hurting one another. This is a pretty good example of how to work with, instead of against, your competitors. Two ice-cream trucks on the same route could lead to hard feelings and trouble, but shift your emphasis and things work out.

You can be driven to your mental limits by your competition. I've known business owners who could hardly function because they were so consumed with anger toward their competitors. This attitude is not healthy for you or your business. Go into moonlighting knowing that you will have competitors. Accept the fact that some of them may fight dirty. Come to terms early with how you will react to competition. Mudslinging and name-calling are not the answers.

One of the best ways to deal with competitors is to get to know them. At times, you will have direct competition that you can't work around. This competition doesn't mean you can't work together. No, I'm not suggesting that you enter into a partnership with your competitors. What I'm saying is if you and your competitors are on talking terms, you can make arrangements so that you both win. Let me give you an example.

Let's say that you are moonlighting by creating and selling craft items. So is your closest competitor. The two of you regularly attend craft shows and flea markets to sell what you make. Because neither one of you can be in two places at one time, it seems reasonable that the two of you could establish a route system to work with. For instance, you go to the flea market this weekend while your competitor works a craft show. Next weekend, you take the craft show and your competitor gets the flea market. This schedule keeps the two of you from butting heads at the same point of sale, and you both come out ahead by working together.

Not all your competitors are going to be cooperative. Some will want to see you driven out of business. Don't let this eat at you. If anything, use it as fuel to challenge your competitor. When you go into business for yourself, you must learn to control your emotions and use your energy wisely. Most important, you have to maintain a good mental attitude. This is much of the battle in winning at business.

The Right Combination

Finding the right combination for regular work and moonlighting is not difficult. It may take a little time. You might even have to experiment a bit to figure out what you really want. Take some time. Your job provides you with security. Don't jump into the first moonlighting idea you decide on. Make a decision, examine it, and then think about it for a week. What's one week going to matter? If you still feel good about your decision, go with it. Once you find the right combination, you can enjoy a full and profitable life as a modern moonlighter. To recap, beat burnout by:

- Moonlighting in a field that's different from your day job
- Making time for yourself
- Not getting greedy
- Gambling only what you can afford to lose
- Establishing a balance between work and play
- Not being afraid of competition
- Finding the best combination of regular full-time work and moonlighting

I wish you all the best in your new life as a moonlighter.

FIVE

MAKING THE TRANSITION

16

GOING FROM MOONLIGHT TO DAYLIGHT

If you are a successful moonlighter, there will probably come a time when you wonder if you should quit your day job and strike out on your own. The odds of being able to do this are very good for most people. Owning your own business can fulfill many dreams, and it can be richly rewarding in more ways than one. Being your own boss is a privilege that many people never experience, but you can reach for this golden ring and grasp it. However, deciding to turn your moonlighting work into a full-time, self-supporting business is one that deserves a lot of thought and planning.

Certain things in life are better in moderation. I love pizza, but I wouldn't want to eat it every day of the week. Your moonlighting business might be compared to the pizza. If you love what you do as a moonlighter, it may be because you don't do it full-time. Changing your life so that your moonlighting work is your life's work can be a mistake.

Is there a particular point in time when you should convert from a moonlighter to a full-time business owner? There should be some stage where you have this opportunity, but there is no guarantee that the chance is worth the risk and the complications that go along with being an independent businessperson. Would you be better off if you quit your regular job? You might be, but you have to weigh all aspects of the decision. Can you make more money as an entrepreneur than you can as an employee? It's almost a certainty that you will have the opportunity to make more money working for yourself than you would working for someone else. However, there is always a risk of losing money when you open a business, and this is a risk that you don't take as an employee.

Unfortunately, so many different types of business endeavors and people involved in this world exist that it's impossible to draw a line and call it the jumping-off point. Each individual has to assess limits and risks on a personal basis. I can't tell you exactly what you should do, but I can give you some basic criteria to consider when you decide to go from employee to business owner.

MINIMUM NEEDS

Certain minimum needs must be considered when thinking of quitting your job and becoming a full-time entrepreneur. First of all, don't think that you will be able to work eight hours a day, five days a week, and survive your first year in business. It's much more likely that you will work longer hours than ever before when you crank your moonlighting venture up to a full-time pace.

To open your own full-time business, you need many things. Money is a big need, but you also need customers. Perhaps the most important element for you is courage. Starting a business of your own and quitting your job can be both exciting and frightening. Fortunately, you will get to test the waters as a moonlighter before you jump into a deep hole that you were not expecting. This is one of the major benefits of starting out as a moonlighter.

If you were to quit your job right now and open a business, you would need a lot of cash to guard against the unknown elements that you may face. By starting out as a moonlighter, you can build your business slowly, profitably, and with good direction. Making a mistake as a moonlighter is much easier to take than it would be if you were depending on your moonlighting work to support you fully. Think of your moonlighting as something of an apprenticeship.

Minimal needs for a business venture vary, depending on the type of business that is being opened and operated. Your business may not require much overhead, but if you plan to live on your earnings, you certainly will have to make a predescribed amount of profit. This is a good place to start evaluating when, if ever, to go into a full-time business.

How much money do you need to support yourself? Will you have to start paying for your own insurance benefits if you start a business? Insurance is very expensive, and far too many entrepreneurs underestimate the cost when planning a business budget. You may take the benefits that your employer provides for granted now, but your attitude will change when you start paying the premiums. In addition to health, dental, and disability insurance, you must consider the cost of insuring your business. The insurance for liability coverage is something that you should be used to as a moonlighter, but the rates may go up when you go full-time.

How much money will you have to save to live on as you go from a part-time business to a full-time business? Moonlighters can work only so many hours in addition to their regular employment. Many forms of moonlighting will allow you to make as much, if not more, from part-time work for yourself as you might make work-ing full-time for an employer. Is this the case with your after-hours business? It's impossible for me to predict what your moonlighting income is or will be, but you have to take this fact into considera-tion. Can you work half the normal time and make just as much money? A lot of people can, but it depends on you, your market, and what you're doing. In any case, you have to establish a viable budget for what your cash reserves will need to be.

A major reason why so many small businesses fail each year is that their owners don't have enough money to float them over the rough spots. Moonlighting is much safer than working full-time for yourself. The security of a day job can be used to meet your finan-cial obligations while the money from moonlighting can be used for any number of purposes. As soon as you need all your moon-lighting money to pay your bills, you are at risk, and you'll proba-bly be under a lot of stress.

So what are the minimum needs for jumping into your own business full-time? It all depends on you and your circumstances, but let's outline a few good considerations to keep in mind:

- Have a business plan.
- Make sure you have a market for your services or products.
- Get your start-up costs covered while you are still an employee for someone else.
- Build up a cash reserve to use as a safety net.
- Take insurance costs into consideration.
- Don't start a full-time business until you are comfortable that the business can support you.
- Wait to start full-time in your business until you have worked the bugs out of the business by moonlighting.
- When you make a commitment to go full-time, you have to stay with your commitment.

A Calculated Risk

Going into business for yourself is always a calculated risk. There are few guarantees in life, and even less in business. The best plans can falter and fail. You will have to take risks to get into business for yourself. Risks are associated with many types of moonlighting, but these risks usually can be counterbalanced by the security of a regular job. Once you leave your job, there no longer is any regular paycheck to cash.

Being in business for yourself may not be what you hope it will be. By starting out as a moonlighter, you can get a good idea how your business will run. Until you cut the cord with your employer and dive into your business full-time, however, you won't know the full extent of what to expect. By the time you feel the full pressure, you no longer will have your job to fall back on. This can be an uncomfortable position to find yourself in. Before you quit your job, make sure that you are comfortable with the decision.

Trading Security for Potential

Trading the security of a job for the potential of owning your own business is something that you may regret. Is there any way to know for sure that working for yourself full-time is the best answer to making a living? I don't think so. Being self-employed offers unlimited potential. Business owners are not restricted by salary caps and supervisors. The amount of money that you can make as your own boss is unknown. You might make less than you did at your former job, or you may become quite wealthy.

Many moonlighters feel strong urges to quit their day jobs and to work for themselves exclusively. I chose many years ago to go out on my own. Have I regretted my decision? On numerous occasions, I've wondered why I wasn't working for someone else. When I evaluate my own situation, I come up with the same answers over and over again. I like to be in control of my own destiny, and I like to make my own rules. For this privilege, I've had to pay some heavy prices in terms of time and effort. Has it been worth it? Yes, it's been worth it for me, but I can easily see why many people would return to a regular job.

Are there riches awaiting you on the other side of the employment pasture? They say the grass is always greener on the other side, but it all has to do with your perception. Some of my best financial years have come from moonlighting in conjunction with a job or one of my other businesses. Trying to make all of the money you want at one task can be extremely difficult. It is often easier, and more profitable, to work a job and moonlight than it is to try to make all the money doing one thing. Even if you are already a business owner, there's room to moonlight in a different venture.

MAKING THE MOVE

Making the move from moonlighter to full-timer can be challenging, to say the least. Each person will react to his or her needs and desires differently. A case can be made for staying with a full-time job and moonlighting for as long as you care to. This is a safe route, and it is one that usually is very profitable. The risk of being in business as a moonlighter is minimal, and the returns can be quite lucrative.

Some people, like myself, have a personality that cries out for the freedom of self-employment. It's very difficult for me to work for someone else when I know I reach my potential when working for myself. But, I must admit, there have been many years in my self-employment that would have been much more profitable if I had held a job and moonlighted instead of growing a full-time business of my own.

I doubt if there is ever a right or wrong time to switch from employee status to business owner. If there is, it is certainly different for various people. Before I had children, people told me there was never a right time to have them. I waited late into life to have children, so that I could have my business interest in full swing first, but life threw me some curveballs. My business planning didn't pan out. The tax laws changed in 1986, and the results had a major effect on my real estate deals. Sometimes you just can't plan enough. There comes a time when you have to go for the gold, and you will know it when this time comes.

When should you make the move? Do it when it feels right, but don't rush yourself. If your moonlighting business is successful, you are gaining strength each month that you stay on your regular job. You should not hurry to jump into business for yourself. If there is a time-sensitive reason for making a move, it's probably not a stable move to make. Things that come quickly often go just as fast. Build a strong foundation for your business as a moonlighter and then evolve into being a full-time business owner.

DON'T MAKE THE MOVE AT ALL?

If you are extremely nervous about starting a full-time business, don't make the move at all. Clearly, certain people are not inclined to be business owners. You might be much happier working a night job for an employer. Even if you operate your own moonlighting business, you may find that it feels more comfortable to keep it as a side income rather than as an absolute need. There's nothing wrong with this line of thinking.

Running a full-time business can take a toll on you. Getting into moonlighting might be fun, and you certainly will enjoy the extra money. But transforming your profitable part-time work into your full-time job could ruin your fun. It's nice to be able to earmark a few hundred dollars for a treat and know that it's not money coming out of your daily budget. Making extra money as a moonlighter will give you plenty of financial freedom, but relying on it to support yourself can cause you a great deal of distress. Use moonlighting as a tool to get what you want and to see if you like the idea of being self-employed. Don't feel pressured to turn your night work into your day job.

INDEX